VIKAS KHANNA

INDIAN HARVEST

CLASSIC AND CONTEMPORARY
VEGETARIAN DISHES

BLOOMSBURY

NEW YORK · LONDON · OXFORD · NEW DELHI · SYDNEY

Bloomsbury USA
An imprint of Bloomsbury Publishing Plc

1385 Broadway   50 Bedford Square
New York   London
NY 10018   WC1B 3DP
USA   UK

www.bloomsbury.com

BLOOMSBURY and the Diana logo are trademarks
of Bloomsbury Publishing Plc

First published 2015

Photography: Michael Swamy
Styling: Michael Swamy and Varun Inamdar
Assistants: Ganesh Shedge and Hanif Sheikh
Design: Maninder Singh

ISBN:
HB: 978-1-63286-200-6
ePub: 978-1-63286-201-3

Library of Congress Cataloging-in-Publication
Data has been applied for.

2 4 6 8 10 9 7 5 3 1

Typeset by Sara Stemen
Printed and bound in China by C&C Offset
Printing Co. Ltd

To find out more about our authors and books
visit www.bloomsbury.com. Here you will find
extracts, author interviews, details of forthcoming
events and the option to sign up for our
newsletters.

Bloomsbury books may be purchased for
business or promotional use. For information
on bulk purchases please contact Macmillan
Corporate and Premium Sales Department at
specialmarkets@macmillan.com.

CONTENTS

Hymn to the Mothers

I am fertile like sun, winds, and waters

I flow with rivers, my sacred daughters

I shine when I see my jewel-like crops

I hear the crystals of dews and drops

I walk with pilgrims in search of truth

I run with pride and support my youth

I am hard like stone and soft like silk

I am black like coal and white like milk

I breathe in every fragrance of spice

I am reborn with every grain of rice

I nurture every new seedling that is born

I cry for every un-lived life and mourn

I am the sparrow that sings to the farms

I welcome everyone with my open arms

I am the gentle Earth that is also air

I live in the silent whispers of the prayer

I can sacrifice it all, just to hear your voice

I give peace and love, and that's my choice

I am India, I am Mother India

I welcome the spring with million flowers

I bow to the summer and the sun's powers

I bathe in the warm showers of monsoon

I fall with every leaf of the autumn moon

I surrender to the harsh winter's treason

I will continue to flourish in every season

Dedicated to all my gurus who taught me

how to cook and roll breads and,

most important, they were all vegetarian.

They truly showed me the power of food and love.

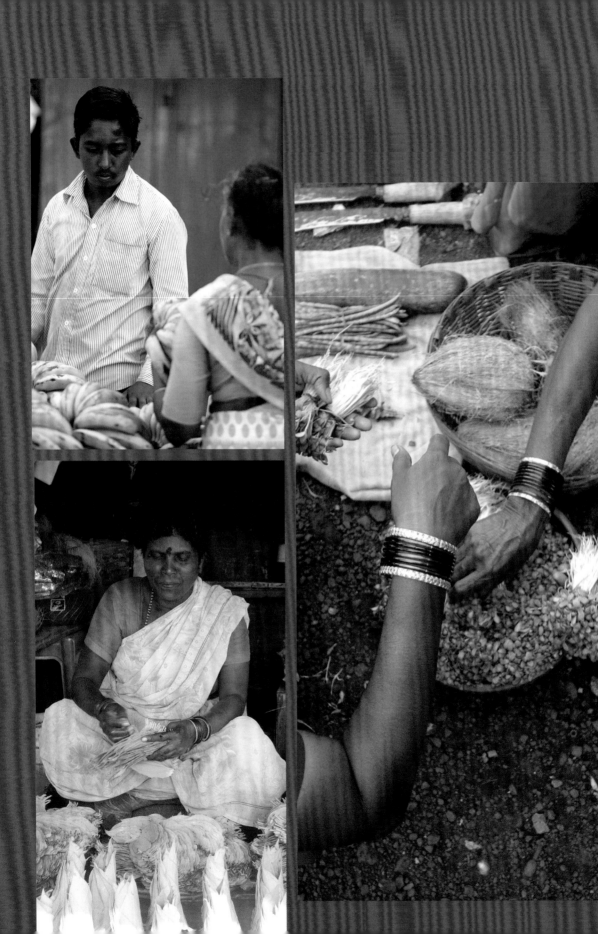

INTRODUCTION

ONE OF MY favorite spaces in the world was our 3-by-10-foot vegetable garden in the backyard of our house in Amritsar, planted and nurtured by my grandmother and me. Aromatic Holy basil, mint, squashes, cilantro, vibrant juicy tomatoes, tangy lemons…I took real pride in my hand-grown herbs and vegetables that I so lovingly tended to each morning and every afternoon when I came back from school. The thrill of rushing home, sometimes with a stolen seedling root pulled out secretly from a neighbor's unattended garden to be replanted in my tiny garden— my own, my very own corner of paradise, which I called the "Temple of Pearls."

I would sit there and see the most beautiful transformations happening every moment. When I would shell a pea, it contained green gems; when I would cut an okra, white rubies would fall on my palm. Sometimes when I saw a squash that had grown high on the rooftop and we had not noticed it was drying, beautiful pearls of life for the next season would be contained within. During winter, wherever I saw mustard growing, I would immediately support it by tying it with a thread to the stick I dug into the ground next to it. The mustard flowers would shine with the reflection of the winter sun. I even grew fenugreek once, and after four months or so it had diamond-shaped yellow seeds sprouting slowly. Nature has its own way of expressing its glory.

The whole process of waiting and watching the seedling slowly break out through the soil, and then the eagerness to finally see its little flowers and fruits, was a delight in itself. One summer morning, years ago, I was woken up by my sister Radhika whose face was glowing. "It's here!" she said with a twinkle in her eyes. In a flash, I was out of bed and both of us ran out to the garden. Panting, we stopped right in front of the tomato plant and there it was—a small, tiny, perfectly round green tomato. For us, it was the best day of the year and the smiles didn't leave our faces all day.

Crowning moments were when freshly plucked mint or perfect ripe tomatoes from my garden made their way to our family table. My chest would overflow with emotion as I oversaw the dinner service with my Biji…handing out second helpings, proudly reminding everyone that the potato curry tasted extra special that night as the cilantro garnish was from "my" vegetable garden. At the same time, though, when I sat down to eat, the spoon never seemed to reach my mouth. Just the thought that I was about to consume something I had so lovingly grown and nurtured with my own hands made me sad. Thus, the best days of the year were always followed by the worst days; and then the plants would bear fruit and the world would be a happy place again.

Every Sunday, I would make my way to the markets shopping for home or for my Banquets—Lawrence Gardens, where the farmers of Punjab would gather, bringing with them an abundance of freshly harvested fruits and vegetables. Those were the days when we would still cook and eat as per the season. Today, in a seasonless world of vegetables and fruits, I sometimes miss the anticipation of choices gifted by the seasons. There is a certain pleasure in eating the vegetables in season—the glistening, firm, and juicy produce gives an extra boost of flavor and color to the recipes we cook.

I suppose it was my small vegetable patch while growing up that gently established my deep connection with Mother Earth—it asks so little of us and in return showers us with its gifts and promises. It inspired me to cook wonderful feasts, to bring natural and combined flavors together with elegant ingredients, give them center stage and design a recipe. As I mix and match the familiar with the unfamiliar, at times I conjure up new taste combinations, a flavorful twist. Other times I simply rely on the tried and tested recipes and techniques handed down over generations.

In present times, all fruits and vegetables are available all year round in many parts of the world, thanks to the technological advances in cultivation and preserving techniques. There is only a handful of produce that can really be called seasonal. This does lead to a greater choice in ingredients at any given time.

Vegetarianism has always been an integral part of the Indian culture, and nowadays is becoming the preferred choice of health-conscious diners. People everywhere are looking to incorporate more vegetables in their meals. In addition to the repertoire of traditional classic vegetarian recipes, there will always remain a need for a taste of something new, something different.

While I was growing up, vegetables were the center point of dining and buying vegetables was a big social event. The vegetables vendor—a small, thin fellow with a booming voice that didn't match his appearance—would come calling out to the Aunty ji to come sample his latest produce.

Aunty ji aaj ki taazi gobi lo, sasti bhi hai
Gaajar shakkar se bhi meethi hai
Mattar ek baar khao, to rooz khaoge
Jaati bahaar ki shalgam hai, le lo achaar bana lena
Aunty ji, jitni sasti subzi main deta hoon, koi nahi de sakta.
Saari Subzi khet se chunke lata hoon.

Aunty ji, do buy this cauliflower! It's fresh and what's more, it's cheap too!
The carrots are sweeter than sugar! And the green peas—you eat them once, you'll eat them every day!
It's your last chance to buy these turnips, so do make a good pickle out of them.
Aunty ji, this reasonable price at which I sell my vegetables, nobody else does! I personally pick and choose them from the farms!!!

So, having sent their husbands and children off to their offices and schools respectively, all the women of the locality would gather around the vegetable vendor. The ladies, with their hair still wet and the fragrance of rose shampoo around them,

would swoop down on the laden cart, while the clever vendor would keep them entertained with his constant chatter. As their expert hands deftly picked the best vegetables (all the time making sure the others didn't lay their hands on those tender beans or those crisp firm cucumbers), they would exchange notes and gossip. Peeping out of the window, unseen and invisible, I would watch this daily ritual with much amusement.

It was a truly spiritual experience to see the reverence these women had for vegetables, and after sometime the whole street would be filled with the aromas of these precious vegetables being cooked. It was the smoke of *tadkas* and the simmering flavors, quietly nurturing us with a shift from the subtle and understated to the bold and bright.

In this book, vegetables are the star ingredients of recipes that showcase their natural sweetness and hidden complexities. Bursting with flavor and infinite colors, the nutritious wholesomeness of these vegetables can be enjoyed as a main course or as a side dish. The recipes are flexible, and most often you will be able to substitute vegetables and herbs for your preferred choice quite easily. Let this process of food preparation be one that gives you joy and the pure simple pleasure of creating with these beautiful and sensuous ingredients. Be prepared for healthy, warm, and comforting meals no matter what the occasion is.

Though as kids we did not like many vegetables, here I have attempted to create new favorites that will surprise all your friends and family. This is a great book in which your creativity is the best recipe. Once you bring your own vision to new creations, you will be pleasantly surprised when you make your own versions. Many vegetables are easy to substitute with just a little change in the cooking time and method. It's truly inspiring that even today our chefs from Junoon visit Union Square Farmer's Market in New York on many days of the week, finding new ingredients and loving the magic of seasons. The aromas of the earth and all the fruits-vegetables-herbs follow me as I walk behind them, thinking of all those women in my life—my Biji, my mom, my aunts—behind whom I once walked through the crowded vegetable markets of India. I think of my garden, my own "Temple of Pearls" that introduced me to the joy and excitement of growing vegetables, fruits, and herbs—and of gently growing life.

SPICE BOX OF
INDIAN KITCHEN

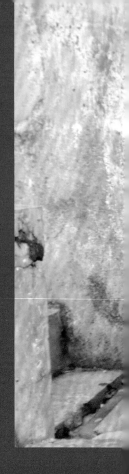

SPICES: There is something still very mystical occurring when I open my spice box and begin the ritual of cooking. These fragrant, smoky, seductive spices softly fill the room with their magic. They are the reason why I am in the kitchen. A small bite of cumin seed while eating a vegetable curry or the strong woody aroma of carom seeds while enjoying a hot puffed bread—it is these little hints of flavors that give Indian cuisine its true identity.

SOUL OF SOIL

I would close my eyes as I inhaled the smoke of wood-roasted sweet potatoes coming from the street vendor passing by my house. It was the time of silent quiet winters. Soon after, another vendor would pass by selling piles of peanuts—a small earthen pot filled with slowly burning mango wood to keep the peanuts warm.

Observing the pace of winters in India is like gazing at the pendulum of an old British clock. Slowly and steadily time passes by. Suddenly the night falls and everything begins to disappear into the quiet fog.

Something about the winter evenings is very calming. The sudden transition of fall to winter is festive and at the same time it seems like the soil hibernates. Everything is about resting in the warm sun and then letting the day pass into the foggy evening.

"Soil is resting," I would feel. Sometimes the dew would freeze and turn into crystals and rest nestled between the grass blades or on top of leaves and everything would come to a standstill. The trees stood there motionless as the last leaves fell to the soil. I would miss the fragrance of the soil. The only color in the garden would be the chrysanthemums in small pots that blossomed like fire balls of rainbow colors.

Then suddenly the soil would show her magical memory and I would see small white-pink petals randomly blossoming from a branch of an apple tree. What was taken away during the harsh winters came back to life, even the singing birds.

The first tiny blades of grass would begin to spread the green carpet and simmer with green brilliance as a welcome to spring. The warm shades of trees begin to shelter the new buds of colors everywhere.

And suddenly we all begin to realize how much we missed the spring.

The soil shows its wonders once again.

IN SEARCH OF SPICES

It is an absolute fact that the search for spices has galvanized an extraordinary discovery of new lands and worlds. It is because of these humble spices that wars were fought, empires destroyed, new dynasties built, and the destiny of mankind changed forever.

But even today they are a source of mystery and myth in most parts of the Western world. It is believed that growing a spice requires a perfect combination of soil structure, sun, and, most important, the soul of the earth.

On another note, it is the silent bite of the spice that fills your mind with memories of a faraway place and makes you rethink how the food would taste without these gifts of flavor from heaven.

Whenever I cooked on the stove as a child, behind the women of the family, I watched them with great reverence when they added a little spice that totally changed the character of the vegetables and gave a quietly veiled reference which seduced me with never-ending surprises.

ANNATTO

The beautiful clusters of annatto hang peacefully like heart-shaped Diwali or Christmas lights.

But the beauty of nature is at its height when you lightly squeeze the pods and out pop the red seeds, which along with the flesh are the main source of the bright yellow-golden color in curries, butters, cheeses, beverages, meats, and more.

Its wonderful earthy peppery flavor and color make it one of the best substitutes for saffron.

ASAFOETIDA FLOWER

The true miracle of nature and creation is da Vinci's *Vitruvian Man*; his study revealed to him that everything in nature was balanced and proportionately connected.

I still remember the day I was traveling to a spice farm to see the asafoetida tree.

Asafoetida is the strongest-smelling spice used in Indian cooking. Its pungent garlicky aroma remains in the mind for the longest time. But what I discovered when I first held the asafoetida flower would have surprised even da Vinci. The beautiful, fragrant, and well-proportioned flower was a far cry from the sticking gum. With bright yellow flowers, it smelled as wonderful as some of best fragrant flowers, such as jasmine or fresh lavender, that fill the air and our gardens with their perfume.

GREEN PEPPERCORN

During the Middle Ages, the peppercorns were worth more than their weight in gold. Individual peppercorns were widely accepted in place of currency in the marketplace. In Dutch, peperduur means "as expensive as peppercorn."

Green peppercorns are a delight to see, growing in a cluster on vines. They are the delicately flavored unripe berries that are usually found preserved in brine or dried, as they are extremely perishable. These green peppercorns are further processed to make black pepper.

PIPPALI

We used to have a container of Chyawanprash sitting on the dining table in our home throughout winter. Right after breakfast our grandfather would remind us kids to eat a spoonful of it. As I scooped this glistening, fragrant, and sticky jam out of the white plastic jar, I wished I would never have to eat it ever again. But as I grew older, it became one of my favorite parts of eating breakfast before leaving home. The mixture of spices combine to make up one of the best Ayurvedic health boosters. Pippali is one of the most important ingredients of this healthy mixture that rejuvenates and nourishes the body. Its aroma is reminiscent of the incense burned in the temples. Its hot earthy flavor is similar to whole black peppercorns, and is best ground or whole.

WILL CARDAMOM GROW?

All kids who grow up in Punjab hear this story time and again. Punjab is the land of fertile plains and there are five rivers that combine to create this soil. There is a folk tale that the soil of Punjab gives birth to gold- and jewel-like crops. This belief led me on a new journey.

Though cardamom is used a lot in Indian cuisine, truly speaking we never used cardamom in our homecooking. A rare exception would be festivals or when the son-in-law of the family or a very special guest was visiting, thanks to it being such an expensive spice. Though I confess I never used it much in everyday cooking, each time I inhaled the aroma of it, I would realize how much I missed it. I distinctly remember that it was stored in a small brass container with a very tight lid. Whenever I got a chance, I stole a pod and ran to my garden to sprinkle it on one marked spot and then waited every day to see the blossom. I would come back from school and inspect my crop; nothing ever happened and I lost the belief in the fertility story. Many many years later I visited a spice farm in Kerala and saw the orchid-like cardamom flower. So fragile, so delicate. Its beauty was breathtaking and made me appreciate it and at the same time be happy that it does not grow everywhere.

STAR ANISE

The regal appearance of the star anise has graced many of my recipes over the years. If God was Michelangelo, this spice would be the ceiling of the Sistine Chapel in his garden. A lot of work has to be done before plucking the spice.

The fresh star anise on the branches of the tree resemble small green stars and are handpicked from 10-to-15-foot high trees in March and April. They are then spread out and sun dried until they turn a rusty brown color and become infused with intense licorice flavor. This intoxicating spice is an integral part of the Chinese five-spice mix.

In some regional cuisines of India, it is also used in garam masala.

STONEFLOWER

In the Chettinad region of Tamil Nadu in South India, known for its vibrant cuisine and architecture of its mansions, one essential spice of their masalas is the stoneflower.

A dry, soft, brown-white-and-black edible lichen, this spice has a woody smell and holistic flavor and is known as kalpasi. To get the full impact of the flavor of this spice, it is best to roast it dry or in a little oil. It adds a great taste to marinades and mixtures.

I have also used stoneflower to make vegetable stock, where the spice invariably adds a new dimension of flavor to the food.

TRIPHAL

On my visit to Goa, I brought back a trunkload of freshly harvested green berries of the triphal. The taste of fresh triphal is totally different from the flavor of the sun dried. I let it sun dry until the seeds pop open. Generally, this spice is added toward the end of the cooking process. It adds an intense aroma and distinct lemony peppery flavor. The tingling sensation that it leaves in the mouth lingers for a long time. Also known as Sichuan pepper, there is no real substitute for this spice.

FRESH TURMERIC

In the natural order of things, every spice moves aside when it comes to turmeric.

It is not just a quintessential part of Indian cooking, it is also an essential part of the rituals and festivities in India. A paste of fresh turmeric is applied to the bride and bridegroom on the day before the wedding. It has been used since ancient Vedic times for beauty and as a giver of life. In Jejuri, a district in Pune, for the festival of Somvati Amavasya, devotees make an offering of turmeric powder. Most Indian recipes are incomplete without the gingery orangey flavor of turmeric.

NUTMEG

While in the Konkan region, I once cracked open a fresh nutmeg fruit—the magenta-pinkish color is so vibrant, it is hard to believe. The leathery shiny texture of mace forms a uniform coating around the nutmeg. Even though the nutmeg and mace grow together, their flavors are completely different; while mace is spicier and pungent, nutmeg has a subtle sweetness.

When the nutmeg matures, it cracks open to reveal the red mace, which turns brownish when dried. In Grenada, the outer pericarp (or the fleshy part covering the nutmeg) is used in making jams and syrups, and in the Konkan region it is also used in making pickles.

CLOVE BLOSSOM

"Nip it in the bud"—these were the words that a farmer said to me about the clove blossoms. The trick is to harvest them just before they blossom in order to get perfect buds. When the blossoms turn pink, that is the right time to pick them. Generally, I use dried cloves in ground form or as a part of bouquet garni, but I have cooked with the clove flower after it has blossomed and it has a milder, subtle, and extremely delicate taste.

Though I was happy harvesting the perfect cloves, the real joy was in seeing clove blossoms transform into a shape similar to fiber-optic lights.

STARTERS

Baby Asparagus
with Star Anise and Sour Cream

The luscious and velvety sour cream lends a wonderful contrast of textures to the crispy asparagus and onions. You can also use hung yogurt instead of sour cream for similar results. Thick or thin asparagus is a preference. Thin asparagus has a tender crisp center, a bold earthiness, and it cooks quickly. It doesn't need to be peeled, unlike the thick variety.

SERVES 4
8 ounces thin baby asparagus
2 tablespoons vegetable oil
3 to 4 whole star anise
1 cup sour cream
Salt to taste
1 tablespoon butter
Freshly ground black pepper to taste
1 medium red onion, thinly sliced

In a medium pot of boiling water, add asparagus and cook for 2 to 3 minutes. Drain and keep warm.

In a medium saucepan, heat the oil on medium heat and gently add the star anise. Cook, stirring until very fragrant, about 2 to 3 minutes. Add the sour cream, salt, butter, and pepper and cook gently until mixture is warm.

Add the asparagus and onions and serve immediately.

Garlicky Spinach with Mushrooms

Exotic shiitake mushrooms with their rich smokiness are regarded as a symbol of longevity and prized for their health benefits, in addition to their delicious taste. Garlic and lemon help in adding a refreshing, robust flavor to the mushrooms and spinach. You can substitute spinach with any other greens like mustard or kale.

SERVES 4
2 tablespoons vegetable oil
6 cloves garlic, thinly sliced
8 ounces shiitake mushrooms, thinly sliced
2 tablespoons lemon juice
1 pound spinach, rinsed and drained
6 to 8 cherry tomatoes, halved
Salt to taste
Freshly ground black pepper to taste

Heat the oil in a medium sized saucepan over medium heat. Cook the garlic until lightly golden, about 2 to 3 minutes. Gently remove half the fried garlic onto a paper towel and reserve for garnish.

Add the mushrooms to the saucepan with the lemon juice and cook for 2 to 3 minutes, stirring occasionally, until soft.

Add the spinach and cherry tomatoes. Cook until the spinach is soft and the mixture is slightly dry, about 2 to 3 minutes.

Season with the salt and pepper and serve hot, garnished with the fried garlic.

Spicy Potato Wedges
with Cumin and Tamarind

This recipe for potato wedges is an excellent and healthy substitute for french fries—here the wedges are baked instead of deep-fried. Adding the sweet-and-sour taste of tamarind makes this dish an unforgettable delight. The smokiness of the cumin is always a welcome flavor. An easy dish to make, it only takes two steps and could be prepared well in advance for easy entertaining.

SERVES 4 TO 6
3 tablespoons vegetable oil
1 teaspoon cayenne pepper, or to taste
1 teaspoon cumin seeds
2 cloves garlic, finely chopped
One 1-inch fresh ginger, peeled and finely chopped
3 tablespoons tamarind paste
Salt to taste
2 pounds large potatoes, scrubbed and each cut into 8 wedges with skins
Fresh cilantro for garnish

Preheat oven to 425°F.

In a large mixing bowl, combine 2 tablespoons vegetable oil, cayenne pepper, cumin seeds, garlic, ginger, tamarind paste, and salt. Add the potato wedges and mix well, until potatoes are evenly coated.

Evenly grease a baking sheet with the remaining oil and place the seasoned wedges in a single layer. Bake the wedges for 35 to 40 minutes until they are crisp and golden, turning them once or twice to ensure even baking.

Serve hot, garnished with the cilantro.

Slow Cooked Yams with Apples

This brings back memories of the festive family tables where I cooked these in large quantities. You can make this dish hot by adding chili flakes or powder, imparting a beautiful yet contrasting flavor of pungency, combined with the sweetness of yams and apple. Sweet potatoes are commonly used in place of yams, as they are more easily available and similar in taste and texture. Yams should be thoroughly scrubbed before cooking.

SERVES 4 TO 6
1 pound yams, peeled and thinly cut into wedges
10 to 12 shallots, peeled
Salt to taste
1 tablespoon ground cumin seeds
2 cloves garlic, crushed
2 apples, thinly cut into wedges
1½ cups vegetable stock
2 rosemary sprigs, coarsely chopped

Preheat oven to 350°F.

Gently toss the yams, shallots, salt, cumin, garlic, and apples in a medium mixing bowl. Arrange in layers in a shallow, ovenproof baking dish.

Evenly pour the vegetable stock over the yam mixture. Bake until the top is browned and the yams are soft and cooked thoroughly, about 1 to 1½ hours.

Serve hot, garnished with the rosemary.

BOW TO THE SOIL

November is a great time for India; festival season is in full blossom. The illustrations of earthen lamps are a part of every greeting card and the nation is overloaded with sweets. My banquets were always overbooked for the celebrations at this time. It was the same every year, except for the year 2000 when I decided to pack my bags and head to the United States. I remember what Morgan Freeman said in *Shawshank Redemption*, "I think it's the excitement only a free man can feel; a free man at the start of a long journey whose conclusion is uncertain."

As I was about to leave, there was an uncertainty about everything. My life was settled in Amritsar—more than I had wished for, more than I ever wanted. But it was more a call from destiny.

As I was standing at the front door of my house, all set to leave, my Biji came and gave me sugar crystals. She stood motionless and just said one line to me—"Mitti di laaj rakhi." Even today those words resonate in my heart.

I don't know the exact translation, but it roughly means "Honor the soil."

Biji had said something very important in just one line. I could not understand the depth of her statement for years. I was trying to survive, trying to keep myself going. How do I honor the soil now? However, many years later, when I made *True Business*, a documentary on Sikhism and a part of the Holy Kitchens series, she said, "Thank you." I hope she meant that I had honored the soil.

In ancient India, when soldiers fought for the nation, their mothers put a tilak on their foreheads with soil in honor of the true essence of life, dignity and victory.

Cauliflower with Ginger and Peanuts

The mild and subtle cauliflower gets a new avatar in this simple dish. It's a very good recipe for large groups, especially when you are serving meals buffet style. The creamy cheese dressing along with the crunchy, roasted peanuts is a perfect combination for the cauliflower.

SERVES 6 TO 8
2 small heads cauliflower, cut into florets
Salt to taste
2 tablespoons butter
One 2-inch fresh ginger, peeled and finely chopped
1 teaspoon turmeric
4 scallions, finely sliced
Freshly ground black pepper to taste
½ cup cream cheese
¼ cup roasted peanuts, coarsely crushed

Fill a large pot with water and bring to a boil over medium-high heat. Reduce the heat to medium and add the cauliflower florets and salt to the pot. Cover with a lid and cook until the cauliflower is tender and cooked through, about 8 to 10 minutes. Drain and transfer to a platter and keep warm.

Melt the butter in a saucepan over medium heat. Add ginger, turmeric, and half the scallions and cook, stirring for about a minute.

Season butter with salt and pepper to taste and cook for another minute. Stir in the cream cheese and remove from the heat.

Pour the cream cheese sauce over the cauliflower and serve hot, garnished with the peanuts and reserved scallions.

Beets in Mustard Seeds with White Sauce

The addition of mustard to the white sauce gives this dish a very warm, refreshing flavor. You can add any seasonal vegetable of your choice. You can also roast the beets instead of boiling them. Keep the skin on while boiling, as it helps the beets retain their flavor and keeps the color intact.

SERVES 4
4 medium beets
1 teaspoon vegetable oil
2 teaspoons mustard seeds
1 clove garlic, crushed
3 tablespoons butter
3 tablespoons all-purpose flour
1 cup whole milk
Salt to taste
Freshly ground black pepper to taste
3 to 4 fresh chives, cut into 1-inch pieces

Cover the beets with water in a medium pot and bring to a boil over high heat. Reduce the heat to low and simmer covered until cooked through, about 1 hour. Drain and set aside to cool. Peel the beets and cut into 1-inch cubes.

In a small saucepan, heat the oil, then add mustard seeds and cook until they splutter. Add garlic and cook for another minute, stirring continuously. Remove from heat.

Melt the butter in a medium saucepan over medium heat, stir in the flour, and cook for 1 minute. Slowly add milk and cook, stirring constantly. Add the salt and pepper and cook for another minute. Stir in the mustard seed-garlic mixture.

Add the beets and cook, stirring until the beets are well coated.

Serve hot, garnished with the chives.

Green Beans in Pomegranate-Coconut Sauce

The vibrant color of green beans combines beautifully with the fragrant pomegranate-coconut sauce. Instead of molasses, you can also use fresh pomegranate juice that has been reduced and thickened.

SERVES 4

1 pound green beans, trimmed and cut crosswise
Salt to taste
2 cloves garlic, finely chopped
½ teaspoon minced fresh ginger
2 tablespoons pomegranate molasses
1 can (16 ounces) unsweetened coconut milk
½ teaspoon sugar
Sprigs of mint
½ cup fresh pomegranate seeds

Add the beans and a pinch of salt to water in a medium pot. Bring to a boil over medium-high heat. Reduce the heat and simmer until the beans are tender, about 3 minutes. Drain and reserve the beans.

Combine the garlic, ginger, pomegranate, coconut milk, and sugar in a medium pan over high heat and bring to a boil. Reduce the heat to low and cook until the flavors are well combined, about 2 to 3 minutes.

Toss the beans with the dressing and serve hot, garnished with the mint sprigs and pomegranate seeds.

SOUPS

Cold Vegetable Soup with Yogurt and Cilantro

A refreshingly cool soup that tastes best when tomatoes are ripe and full of natural sweetness, with the jalapeño adding a hint of spiciness. Substituting Greek yogurt for regular yogurt adds velvety creaminess and a lovely tangy flavor. This soup could be made up to two days in advance and is great at summer parties.

SERVES 4 TO 6

1 medium yellow pepper
1 small red onion
2 tablespoons vegetable oil
3 cloves garlic, coarsely chopped
2 pounds ripe tomatoes, seeded and coarsely chopped
1 jalapeño chili, seeded
Salt to taste
¼ cup plain low-fat yogurt
⅓ cup sour cream
4 teaspoons fresh cilantro

Coarsely chop the yellow pepper and onion.

In a heavy-bottom skillet, heat the oil on medium heat. Add the garlic, yellow peppers, red onion, tomatoes, jalapeño, and salt. Cook, stirring occasionally, until the mixture becomes dry and very aromatic, about 4 to 5 minutes. Remove from the heat and let cool at room temperature.

Transfer the mixture to a blender or food processor with knife blade attached. Add the yogurt and process until smooth.

Pour the purée into a bowl, cover, and refrigerate until well chilled, at least 6 hours or overnight.

In a small bowl, combine the sour cream and salt. Cover and refrigerate.

To serve, top soup with sour cream and garnish with the cilantro.

Onion Soup with Ginger and Cumin

A simple savory soup in which the versatility of onions shines as the main ingredient. While pan roasting onions, make sure to occasionally stir them for even caramelization or they will burn and become bitter. Caramelization brings out the sweetness, which adds a wonderful rich flavor to this soup along with the ginger and cumin.

SERVES 4 TO 6
2 tablespoons butter
1 tablespoon olive oil
3 large red onions, each cut in half and thinly sliced
One 2-inch fresh ginger
1 tablespoon cumin seeds
4 cups vegetable broth
Salt to taste
Freshly ground black pepper to taste

In a saucepan, heat the butter and oil over medium-low heat until the butter melts. Add the onions, ginger, and cumin; cover and cook until tender and golden brown, about 25 to 30 minutes, stirring occasionally.

Remove cover and increase the heat to high. Add the broth, salt, and pepper and bring it to a boil. Reduce the heat to low, cover, and simmer for 10 to 15 minutes.

Serve hot with toasted bread.

Fava, Green Bean, and Pea Soup

The light earthiness of fava beans is inherent to this super healthy and nutritious soup full of the colors and flavors of spring. Puréeing half the liquid and then adding it back to the soup helps create the body while retaining the texture of the beans. When in season, I prefer to use fresh, sweet, and tender green beans, fava beans, and peas, but frozen will work just as well.

SERVES 4 TO 6
6 tablespoons vegetable oil
1 medium red onion, chopped
1 clove garlic, chopped
8 ounces thin green beans, cut into 1-inch pieces
12 ounces frozen fava beans, thawed
1 cup frozen peas, thawed
Salt to taste
Freshly ground black pepper to taste
4 cups vegetable stock
10 to 12 cloves
Chives for garnish

Heat 2 tablespoons of oil in a large saucepan over medium-high heat. Add the onion and the garlic and cook until the onions soften, about 4 to 5 minutes. Add the green beans, fava beans, peas, salt, and pepper to the pan and cook, stirring continuously for a minute.

Increase the heat to high and add the stock and bring it to a boil for 5 minutes. Reduce the heat to low and simmer for 10 minutes.

Gently transfer half the hot liquid to a blender or food processor and blend to a purée. Then return it to the pan and keep warm until served.

Heat the remaining oil in a small saucepan over medium-high heat. Remove the oil from the heat, add the cloves, and let it sit at room temperature for a few minutes. Remove cloves.

Serve the soup hot, drizzled with clove oil and the chives.

Creamy Avocado and Coconut Soup

This soup combines amazing flavors—avocado and coconut, along with the very light, lemony flavor of cilantro. The creaminess of this soup comes from the smooth textures of avocado, yogurt, and coconut milk. No cream is added, making it light and healthy. A cool, refreshing soup that can be served on any occasion.

SERVES 4

1 clove garlic, crushed
1 fresh green chili, seeded and chopped
½ cup roughly chopped fresh cilantro
2 medium avocados, halved, pitted, and coarsely chopped
1 cup plain yogurt
2 cups coconut milk
1 tablespoon olive oil
Pinch of sugar
Juice of 1 lemon
Salt to taste
1 small tomato, seeded and diced
3 to 4 chives cut into 2-inch pieces

In a blender, add the garlic, chili, cilantro, 1½ avocados, yogurt, coconut milk, olive oil, sugar, and lemon juice and process until smooth. Season with salt and chill for a few hours, covered in the refrigerator.

Serve chilled, garnished with the reserved avocados, tomato, and chives.

Beet and Yogurt Soup

A great comforting winter soup, especially when there is a surplus of root vegetables. The potatoes add a very nice creamy texture and thickness while the earthy flavor and vibrant ruby red color come from the beets. Garnishing with yogurt swirls adds to the presentation.

SERVES 6

2 tablespoons olive oil
1 teaspoon cumin seeds
1 teaspoon coriander seeds
1 pound beets, peeled and chopped
1 cup chopped onions
1 small red pepper, seeded and chopped
1 large potato, peeled and chopped
4 cups vegetable stock
Salt to taste
Freshly ground black pepper to taste
½ cup low-fat yogurt, whisked until smooth
¼ cup pea shoot leaves

Heat the oil in a heavy-bottom skillet on medium-high heat. Add the cumin, coriander, beets, onions, pepper, and potato and cook until very fragrant, about 3 to 4 minutes.

Add the stock, salt, and pepper and bring it to a boil.

Cover the pan, reduce the heat to low, and simmer for 15 to 20 minutes, until the vegetables are cooked through. Gently transfer the mixture to a blender or a food processor and blend to a purée in batches.

Pour the soup into bowls and garnish with swirls of yogurt and chives.

LOST SOIL

The banquet halls of Lawrence Gardens, our catering business, were built in the rear of our house—a space that was originally a garden.

It was the place where my brother, sister, cousins, and I would spend our time—playing or just lying in the sun.

This was the same soil that once nurtured my favorite mango tree and sometimes in summer gave us the most fragrant mint leaves. It gave us perfect turnips in winter and our most treasured pumpkins in the autumn.

As the business began to flourish, and we started having more parties, the grass started dying because of the excessive foot traffic. And when it rained, there would be muddy puddles everywhere. We would use jute bags to level the ground.

We even had to cut down the silent mango tree and my favorite lime tree that was hiding in the corner to make more space for the banquet facilities.

Before we knew it, the entire garden was gone and we decided to cover it with kota stone.

It did not seem to be a big deal at that time; rather a sheer business decision. However, within a few days, everything began to change. No more birds coming to visit us; no more soft tender dew-laden grass under our bare feet; and no more "surprise" mangoes in the morning, fallen to the ground.

It was a need for survival, but we lost more in that deal—we lost our soil.

Cheesy Broccoli Nutmeg Soup

A thick creamy soup that takes the natural flavors of broccoli to another level. This is an example of how simple cooking can be so effective. A dash of warm, freshly grated nutmeg complements the cheese. When puréeing the soup, always process it in small batches, very cautiously, so that the soup does not spill out.

SERVES 4
20 ounces broccoli, broken into florets
1 medium red onion, coarsely chopped
1½ cups vegetable stock
1½ cups whole milk
Salt to taste
Freshly ground black pepper to taste
⅔ cup grated cheddar cheese
Pinch of freshly grated nutmeg

Combine the broccoli, onion, and stock in a large saucepan over high heat. Bring to a boil, cover, and reduce the heat to low and simmer for 10 minutes or until the florets are tender.

Gently transfer the mixture to a blender or a food processor and blend to a purée in batches.

Return the soup to the pan and add the milk, salt, and pepper and bring to a boil on high heat. Reduce the heat to low and simmer for about 3 to 5 minutes until all the flavors are well combined. Stir in the cheese and simmer for 2 to 3 minutes, stirring occasionally, until the cheese melts and the soup thickens slightly.

Serve hot, seasoned with the nutmeg.

Zucchini and Spinach Soup

For me this is not just a soup, it is a hearty meal—great any time of the year. You can substitute zucchini with any kind of squash and still get amazing results. Aromatic turmeric has been used in Indian cuisine for centuries for flavor as well as for its healing properties. Adding it to soups, as in this recipe, is a great way to include turmeric in your meals. I often add boiled lentils or pulses to this recipe, and with a piece of any warm crusty bread it works like a complete meal for me.

SERVES 4
2 tablespoons vegetable oil
2 cloves garlic, coarsely chopped
½ teaspoon turmeric
2 medium tomatoes, coarsely chopped
3 cups vegetable stock
2 pounds zucchini, cut into 1-inch pieces
Salt to taste
1 large bunch spinach, rinsed and chopped
Juice of 1 lemon

Heat the oil in a large saucepan over low heat and cook the garlic, turmeric, and tomatoes until the tomatoes are soft, about 4 minutes.

Increase the heat to high and add the stock, zucchini, and salt and bring to a boil. Reduce the heat and simmer covered for about 15 minutes. Add the spinach, stir, and remove the pan from heat.

Stir in the lemon juice and serve hot.

Cool Cucumber-Dill Soup

Cucumber is a great reminder that summer has arrived. When combined with the cooling yogurt, it creates a very refreshing effect on the throat and mind. Dill adds a wonderful contrasting flavor to the crisp cucumber and fresh mint. Small portions of this chilled soup are a perfect starter to a great summertime meal—light and healthy.

SERVES 4
1 large cucumber, peeled and cut into ½-inch pieces
4 tablespoons chopped dill
2 cups plain yogurt
1 cup whole milk
Salt to taste
Sprigs of mint for garnish
1 teaspoon cayenne pepper

In a large bowl, combine the cucumber, dill, yogurt, milk, and salt until well mixed. Cover and refrigerate for at least 2 hours.

Divide the soup into the 4 chilled bowls, garnished with the mint and cayenne pepper.

Yam Soup with Cilantro and Fennel Seeds

The sweetness of yam combines delightfully with the licorice flavor of fennel seeds, making this an all-time favorite. The silky texture is enhanced by a hint of spiciness from chilies and aromatic spices such as cumin. You can substitute milk or yogurt in place of heavy cream for a healthier version.

SERVES 4 TO 6
1 tablespoon sunflower oil
1 medium onion, finely chopped
One 1-inch fresh ginger, peeled and coarsely chopped
2 cloves garlic
1 teaspoon ground cumin seeds
½ teaspoon turmeric
1 pound yam, peeled and cut into small pieces
1 tablespoon fennel seeds
2 teaspoons red chili powder
1 green chili, such as Thai chili, seeded and coarsely chopped
Salt to taste
3 cups vegetable stock
1 cup heavy cream
1 tablespoon vegetable oil
Sprigs of fresh cilantro

Heat the oil in a large saucepan over medium-high heat. Add the onions, ginger, and garlic and cook until the onions are soft, about 3 to 4 minutes. Add cumin, turmeric, yams, fennel seeds, ½ teaspoon chili, and salt and cook, stirring continuously until the flavors are well blended. Pour in the stock and increase the heat to high and bring it to a boil.

Reduce the heat to low and simmer covered until the yams are cooked through, about 15 to 20 minutes. Remove from the heat and stir in the cream.

Gently transfer the mixture to a blender or a food processor and purée in batches.

Heat the vegetable oil on medium heat. Remove from the heat. Add remaining chili powder and set it aside.

Serve warm, garnished with sprigs of cilantro and chili oil.

Winter Pumpkin and Rice Soup

Pumpkin is the quintessential ingredient for fall going into winter. This sweet and savory soup is a perfect blend of the sweet, warm, and comforting flavors of pumpkin. For me, this is a perfect soup recipe and when made with seasonal vegetables and combined with rice is a complete meal. You can also add your favorite cheese to give it a dense flavor.

SERVES 6
2 tablespoons olive oil
2 medium red onions, finely chopped
1 teaspoon curry powder
1 pound pumpkin, peeled, seeded, and cubed
2 cloves garlic, finely chopped
1 fresh green chili, seeded and finely chopped
Salt to taste
1 cup long grain basmati rice, rinsed
4 cups vegetable stock, plus more as needed

Heat the oil in a large saucepan over medium heat. Add the onion and curry powder, and cook until onions soften, about 4 to 5 minutes. Add the pumpkin, garlic, chili, salt, and rice and cook, stirring continuously until the pumpkin becomes mushy, about 5 to 7 minutes.

Pour in the stock and bring to a boil. Reduce the heat, cover, and simmer for about 10 to 12 minutes until the rice and pumpkins are soft and all the flavors are well combined.

Serve hot.

SALADS

Mixed Bean Salad with Orange Vinaigrette

Vinaigrette is one of the most versatile dressings. Extra-virgin olive oil adds a very rich flavor but if you prefer a milder dressing, you can substitute it with vegetable or canola oil. You can also use steamed vegetables with this dressing and achieve excellent results.

SERVES 6 TO 8
8 ounces green beans, trimmed and cut into 1-inch pieces
1 can (15 ounces) garbanzo beans, rinsed and drained
1 can (15 ounces) black beans, rinsed and drained
1 can (15 ounces) red kidney beans, rinsed and drained
3 cherry tomatoes, cut into quarters
1 orange, segmented

FOR THE VINAIGRETTE
1 teaspoon Dijon mustard
3 tablespoons red wine vinegar
½ cup extra-virgin olive oil
¼ cup freshly squeezed orange juice
1 small shallot, minced
Salt to taste
1 teaspoon sugar
Freshly ground black pepper to taste

In a medium saucepan, boil 1 inch of water over high heat.

Add the green beans and return to a boil. Reduce the heat to low and simmer until beans are tender crisp, about 3 to 4 minutes. Drain the beans. Rinse with cold water, drain, and transfer the beans to a large serving bowl.

Mix in the garbanzo beans, black beans, red beans, and tomatoes.

For the vinaigrette, whisk the mustard and vinegar together until creamy. Slowly add the oil in a steady stream, whisking constantly until the oil is well combined and the dressing is emulsified. Add the orange juice, shallot, salt, sugar, and pepper and mix well.

Add the vinaigrette to the beans and toss to coat evenly.

Cover and refrigerate at least an hour, and up to 8 hours, before serving. Garnish with the orange segments.

Fennel Slaw and Melon Balls

Fennel adds a wonderful flavor of licorice while melon adds a contrasting juicy sweet undertone. The sweetness of honey and the smoky flavor of roasted cumin is enhanced by the oil and vinegar emulsion.

SERVES 4

½ **small honeydew melon, seeded**
3 tablespoons vegetable oil
3 tablespoons red wine vinegar
1 teaspoon Dijon mustard
1 teaspoon honey
1 teaspoon lightly roasted cumin seeds, ground
Salt to taste
Freshly ground black pepper to taste
1 medium fennel bulb, trimmed and thinly sliced
2 tablespoons dill leaves

Using a melon baller, scoop out the flesh of the honeydew and transfer it to a mixing bowl.

In a medium bowl, whisk together the oil, vinegar, mustard, honey, cumin, salt, and pepper until smooth and creamy. Add the melon balls and fennel and toss to coat evenly with the dressing.

Serve immediately, garnished with the dill.

Roasted Corn Salad with Lemon and Avocado

After you grill the corn and add it to your salad, you will discover a whole new flavor of charred corn. This simple and easy-to-make recipe can be made in large quantities and can also be used as stuffing in wraps.

SERVES 4
2 ears corn
1 medium tomato, cut into ½-inch pieces
2 tablespoons coarsely chopped mint
2 tablespoons fresh lemon juice
1 tablespoon olive oil
Salt to taste
1 teaspoon chili flakes
¼ teaspoon sugar
1 ripe medium avocado, seeded and peeled, cut into ½-inch pieces

Lightly grease and preheat a grill on high. Peel back the corn husks and remove the silk. Place the prepared corn on the grill and cook until the corn is lightly charred and aromatic, about 8 to 12 minutes. Gently remove the corn from the cob and slice off the kernels. Transfer the corn to a large mixing bowl.

Add the tomato, mint, lemon juice, oil, salt, chili flakes, and sugar.

Serve the salad tossed with the avocado pieces.

Daikon Radish Salad with Tomatoes and Peanuts

The presentation of this dish is always a crowd-pleaser and is also very convenient when serving to large groups. The pungent flavor of daikon works very well with the lemony onion-tomato salsa, while the roasted peanuts add a great texture.

SERVES 4

3 large daikon radishes
1 small red onion, finely chopped
2 large ripe tomatoes, seeded and finely chopped
3 tablespoons finely chopped fresh cilantro
Juice of 1 lemon
2 green chilies, finely chopped
Salt to taste
2 tablespoons peanuts, roasted
1 lime, cut into wedges

Cut the diakon radishes into 1-inch cubes. Using a lemon baller, gently scoop out a bowl in the center of each cube.

In a medium mixing bowl, combine the onion, tomatoes, cilantro, lemon juice, chilies, and salt and mix until all the flavors are well blended.

Place a layer of peanuts at the bottom of the scooped daikon. Using a teaspoon, top it with the onion-tomato mixture and serve immediately with the lime wedges.

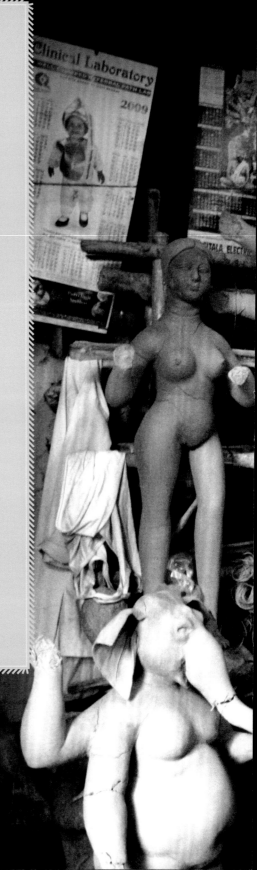

MOTHER OF SOIL

Once when I was watching *Devdas*, a Bollywood classic based on the book by renowned Bengali writer Sarat Chandra Chattopadhyay, I recalled the story of the clay used to make Mother Durga's idols during the *Puja*.

Durga Puja, regarded as one of the most prominent Hindu festivals in India, is typically a festival of eastern India. The soil being a symbol of immortality, creation, and power, the idols of Durga are made with a mixture that is combined with the clay from the doorsteps of courtesans and from the banks of the Ganges.

Thus originated the little-known but age-old custom of collecting a handful of soil (*punya mati*) from the *nishiddho pallis* of Kolkata, literally meaning "forbidden territories"—the brothels—and adding it to the clay mixture that goes into the making of the Durga idols.

A few years ago I went to Kolkata during the festival and truly understood the meaning of this ritual. Mother Durga is the true embodiment of women's strength, but her divine form is a symbol of fertility and inclusiveness, and thus created with soil.

Potatoes and Raisins with Smoked-Paprika Dressing

If the baby potatoes are too large, then quarter them for this salad. The earthy aroma of paprika and the richness of sour cream lend a wonderful dressing to the potatoes and sweet raisins. I generally make this dressing in large quantities and use it later for spreads and marinades.

SERVES 6
2 pounds baby potatoes, halved
Salt to taste
2 tablespoons sour cream
1 teaspoon stone-ground mustard
2 tablespoons cider vinegar
¼ cup extra-virgin olive oil
Pinch of smoked paprika
1 teaspoon honey
¼ cup raisins
1 medium red onion, thinly sliced
2 tablespoons finely chopped parsley

Place the potatoes in a large pot and cover with cold water. Add a tablespoon of salt and bring it to a boil on high heat. Reduce the heat to low and simmer until the potatoes are tender and cooked through, about 12 to 15 minutes. Drain, cool, and reserve the potatoes.

In a large mixing bowl, combine the sour cream, mustard, vinegar, olive oil, paprika, honey, and salt and mix until all the flavors are merged well.

Add the potatoes, raisins, and onions and toss to combine. Serve chilled, garnished with the parsley.

Crumbled Cheese with Peaches and Pecans

Peaches bring out the subtle sweetness of the crumbled cheese, while the bitterness of the arugula complements the sweet-and-sour tamarind dressing. I like to lightly toast the pecans before adding them to the salad since that intensifies the flavor of the nuts and makes them the perfect crunchy topping for salads.

SERVES 4
1 quart whole milk
4 tablespoons lemon juice
3 peaches, pitted and sliced
1 small bunch arugula, trimmed
¼ cup pecans, lightly toasted
Salt to taste
2 tablespoons tamarind paste
1 tablespoon sugar
1 teaspoon cumin seeds, roasted
1 lime, cut into thin wedges

Bring the milk to a boil and turn off the heat to bring the temperature down to 176°F. Add 1 tablespoon of lemon juice at a time, stirring after every addition until the milk separates. Allow the curds to cool, and then strain the mixture through a cheese cloth. Rinse the curds with fresh water and squeeze to remove the moisture. Transfer the curds to a large mixing bowl. Add the peaches, arugula, pecans, salt, tamarind, sugar, and cumin seeds and gently toss to evenly coat the ingredients.

Serve chilled or at room temperature, garnished with the lime wedges.

Spinach and Mandarin Salad with Almonds

Navel or cara cara oranges work great in this recipe because of their firm texture and wonderful aroma. You can also use any salad green. This recipe oozes citrus flavor, adding to the crunch of almonds. Cider vinegar adds a mild acidic and tart flavor.

SERVES 4

2 tablespoons orange marmalade
1 medium red onion, thinly sliced
2 tablespoons cider vinegar
2 tablespoons olive oil
Salt to taste
1 teaspoon sugar
2 oranges such as navel
1 bunch spinach, about 6 cups
½ cup almonds, lightly toasted

In a medium glass bowl, whisk the marmalade, onions, vinegar, oil, salt, and sugar until smooth and creamy.

With a sharp paring knife, gently cut out the segments of oranges.

Toss the spinach, oranges, and marmalade dressing until well combined.

Serve garnished with the toasted almonds.

MAINS

Bitter Gourd Stuffed with Green Mangoes

The sweet-and-sour tartness of the unripe mango, smoky cumin, and licorice fennel perfectly offset the bitterness of the gourd. Bitter gourd is an extremely popular vegetable in Indian cuisine, partially because of the health benefits it brings to the table. It was one of my grandmother's favorite vegetables.

One of the more popular ways to reduce the bitterness of the gourd is to rub the slices with salt and leave them to rest for 15 to 20 minutes. Rinse them before cooking.

SERVES 4
8 to 10 tender bitter gourds
2 teaspoons ground turmeric
Salt to taste
2 tablespoons vegetable oil, plus more for frying
3 to 4 dried red chilies, broken in half
2 teaspoons fennel seeds, coarsely crushed
2 green mangoes, grated
One 1-inch fresh ginger, peeled and minced
1 green chili, such as serrano, minced
1 teaspoon coriander powder
1 teaspoon cumin powder
Juice of 1 lemon

Cut the tips off the bitter gourds and gently scrape them with the back of a teaspoon. Cut into 2½-to-3-inch rounds resembling cannelloni. Scoop out and remove the seeds with the back of a spoon. Evenly rub them with 1 teaspoon of turmeric and salt. Let them rest for at least 30 minutes at room temperature.

In a medium pan, heat the oil on medium heat. Add the red chilies and cook, stirring for a minute. Remove from the heat and, using a slotted spoon, remove the chilies and reserve for garnish.

Heat the infused oil and add the fennel seeds, grated green mango, ginger, remaining turmeric, green chili, coriander powder, and cumin powder. Cook, stirring continuously until the mixture becomes dry and fragrant, about 4 minutes. Season it with salt and lemon juice. Remove from the heat and keep warm.

Heat the vegetable oil for frying to 350°F.

Gently squeeze the bitter gourd slices and pat them dry with a kitchen towel. Carefully fry them until they are darker in color and slightly crisp.

Remove them with a slotted spoon and drain the excess oil onto a paper towel. Fill the gourd slices with the green mango mixture and serve hot, garnished with fried red chilies.

Chili-Garlic Roasted Cabbage

Roasting is one of the best ways to preserve and enhance the flavors of vegetables. The peppery flavor of the raw cabbage gets sweeter as it cooks. Chili-garlic marinade adds a spicy and bold kick to the simply roasted cabbage. It can be prepared in advance and kept in the refrigerator for up to a week.

SERVES 4
4 tablespoons canola oil, plus more for greasing the baking tray
1 teaspoon mustard seeds
2 tablespoons chili powder
4 cloves garlic, coarsely chopped
2 tablespoons white vinegar
1 tablespoon brown sugar
Salt to taste
1 medium green cabbage, cut into 6 to 8 wedges
Lemon wedges for garnish
3 fresh red chilies, halved
Few sprigs fresh cilantro

Heat the oil in a small pan and fry the mustard seeds on medium heat until they start crackling. Reduce the heat to low and add the chili powder, garlic, vinegar, sugar, and salt and cook, stirring until the mixture becomes thick. Add a tablespoon of water to avoid burning the spices.

Remove from the heat and let it cool.

Preheat the oven to 400°F and evenly grease a baking tray with oil.

In a medium mixing bowl, evenly coat the cabbage with chili-garlic sauce and place it in a single layer on the baking tray.

Roast in the medium rack of the oven about 20 to 25 minutes. Flip halfway through to ensure the cabbage is evenly cooked.

Serve hot, garnish with the lemon wedges, red chilies, and cilantro.

Tamarind-Cumin-Scented Coloca

Tangy, sweet, and spicy—this recipe has a well-rounded balance of flavors
a popular vegetable in cuisines all over India. Each region has its own un
and recipe. While similar in texture to well-done potatoes, colocasia has a
texture and a sweet nutty flavor.

SERVES 4
Salt to taste
12 to 14 ounces colocasia root
2 tablespoons canola oil
2 medium red onions, thinly sliced
3 cloves garlic, crushed
2 teaspoons cumin seeds
2 dried red chilies
1 tablespoon chili powder
2 tablespoons tamarind paste
1 tablespoon brown sugar
¼ cup fresh parsley leaves

In a medium pot with a tight lid, boil 5 cups of salted water on high heat. Add the colocasia roots, cover, and continue to boil until the colocasia is cooked through. Drain and let it cool at room temperature.

Gently peel, cut into halves if the pieces are too large, and reserve.

Heat the oil in a small pan and fry the onions, garlic, cumin, and red chili on medium heat until the onions turn golden on the edges, about 4 to 5 minutes. Add the chili powder, tamarind, sugar, and salt and cook, stirring until the mixture becomes dry and fragrant. Add the reserved colocasia and cook, stirring until well coated. Add 2 tablespoons of water to ensure even coating.

Stir in the parsley and serve hot.

Lotus Root Silky Kofta

A symbol of beauty and purity since ancient times, the lotus flower is largely edible—the flowers, seeds, leaves, and the rhizome. The lotus root has a beautiful lace-like design with tiny holes. It is valued in the culinary world for its mild flavor and crunchy texture. Even in this kofta, lotus root adds a rich, meaty texture and taste, added in a creamy sauce flavored with cardamom, cinnamon, and fennel.

SERVES 4
1 pound tender lotus root, washed and peeled
¼ cup gram flour
Salt to taste
2 green chilies such as serrano or Thai, finely chopped
½ teaspoon grated fresh ginger, chopped
2 tablespoons finely chopped fresh cilantro leaves
Vegetable oil for frying, plus 2 tablespoons
1 tablespoon chili powder
2 red onions, finely sliced
2 cardamom pods, lightly crushed
One 1-inch cinnamon stick
1 teaspoon fennel seeds
1 cup heavy cream

Cut a 3-inch piece of lotus root into roundels, about ⅛-inch thick, and finely grate the remaining lotus root. In a mixing bowl, combine the gram flour, grated lotus root, salt, chilies, ginger, and 1 tablespoon cilantro and knead to a smooth mixture. Add a little water if required. Make 10 to 12 small round balls.

Heat the oil to 350°F and deep-fry the balls in batches until golden. Remove them with a slotted spoon and drain the excess oil onto a paper towel. In the same oil, fry the lotus root roundels until golden brown. Remove with a slotted spoon and drain the excess oil onto the paper towel. Reserve for garnish.

Heat 2 tablespoons oil over medium heat. Remove from heat and add chili powder. Reserve for garnish.

In a medium pot, boil the onions, cardamom, cinnamon, and fennel seeds with 3 cups of water on high heat until the water reduces to half and the mixture becomes thick. Remove from the heat and let it cool at room temperature. Transfer to a blender and process to a smooth paste.

Now shift to a saucepan and bring to a boil on medium heat. Add the cream and season with salt and gently simmer.

Transfer the sauce to a serving dish and arrange the lotus balls over it. Drizzle with chili oil and serve garnished with lotus root chips and cilantro.

Pickled Mushrooms with Bok Choy

A quick and easy stir-fry with crispy bok choy, seasoned with garlic, ginger, and smoked paprika. The tartness of the pickled mushrooms adds a whole new flavor to the dish. The mushrooms can be pickled well in advance and stored for up to a few weeks in the refrigerator. The flavors of the brine can be varied by the addition of spices like chilies and coriander seeds.

SERVES 6
½ **cup white wine vinegar**
Salt to taste
3 tablespoons honey
1 pound button mushrooms, cleaned and halved
3 tablespoons vegetable or sesame oil
2 cloves garlic, minced
One 2-inch fresh ginger, peeled and grated
2 dried chilies, broken in half
1 pound baby bok choy, trimmed
1 teaspoon soy sauce
½ **teaspoon smoked paprika**
2 tablespoons sesame seeds, lightly toasted

In a small saucepan, heat the vinegar, salt, and honey over medium heat until warm, about 2 minutes. Remove from the heat, add the mushrooms, and leave to marinate for at least an hour.

Drain the liquid and reserve the mushrooms.

Heat the oil in a wok on medium high heat. Add the garlic, ginger, and dried chili and cook, stirring until fragrant, about 2 minutes.

Add the bok choy, soy sauce, salt, and paprika and stir until the bok choy is cooked. Add the reserved mushrooms and continue to cook until all the flavors have combined well.

Serve hot, sprinkled with the sesame seeds.

Okra with Yogurt Garlic Curry

This delicious yogurt curry dish is made with crispy okra, but just about any seasonal vegetable tastes great when added to this versatile curry. A bowl of this steaming hot, sour, and spicy dish, along with rice and pickles, makes for the perfect comfort food any time of the day or year.

SERVES 4 TO 6
Vegetable oil for frying
2 pounds tender okra, trimmed and slit vertically
1 cup plain yogurt
2 tablespoons gram flour
3 tablespoons mustard oil
1 red onion, chopped
3 cloves garlic, chopped
1 green chili such as serrano, chopped
1 teaspoon black cumin seeds
1 teaspoon ground turmeric
Salt to taste
2 fresh red chilies, halved

Heat the oil to 350°F.

Fry the okra in batches until cooked through. Remove with a slotted spoon and drain the excess oil onto a paper towel.

In a mixing bowl, whisk together the yogurt and gram flour into a smooth batter and reserve.

Smoke the mustard oil on high heat in a skillet and then reduce the heat to medium. Add the onion, garlic, green chili, black cumin, turmeric, and salt and cook, stirring continuously until all flavors are well combined.

Add the yogurt mixture and bring to a boil. Continue to cook until the mixture is smooth and thick, about 3 to 4 minutes.

Serve hot with the okra, garnished with the red chilies.

Purple Yams in Cabbage Parcels

I was first introduced to stuffed cabbage parcels at Veselka—a popular Ukrainian restaurant in Manhattan. In Eastern European countries, stuffed cabbage is a staple comfort food. Made with a variety of fillings, usually meat, it can be simmered in a broth or sauce, baked, or just steamed. Here the parcels are steamed with a filling of sweet-savory purple yams. Any variety of cabbage will work in this recipe—green, savoy, or even red. Choose cabbage with large, firm, unblemished leaves.

SERVES 8
2 tablespoons oil
Pinch of asafoetida
1 teaspoon mustard seeds
One 1-inch fresh ginger, chopped
2 green chilies, chopped
1 pound purple yams, boiled, peeled, and cut into 1-inch cubes
2 tablespoons grated jaggery
Salt to taste
1 teaspoon dried mango powder
1 teaspoon coarsely ground pippali pepper
3 tablespoons finely chopped fresh cilantro
8 large cabbage leaves
8 scallions, root end trimmed, to tie the parcels (optional)

Heat the oil in a skillet on medium heat and add asafoetida, mustard seeds, ginger, and chilies and fry, stirring until fragrant, about 1 minute. Add yams, jaggery, and salt and continue to cook until the yams are evenly coated with the spices.

Stir in the mango powder, pippali, and cilantro and remove from the heat. Divide the mixture between the cabbage leaves. Gently fold them into parcels and secure with cocktail sticks, toothpicks, or scallions. Using a steamer, steam them for 10 minutes until soft.

Serve immediately.

Spiced Cauliflower with Orange Sauce

Orange has one of the most refreshing flavors and adds a balanced yet vibrant taste and aroma to the crispy cauliflower. Caramelized onions add a nice savory bite to the tangy tomato-orange sauce. Alternatively, the cauliflower can be roasted to make a healthier version of this dish.

SERVES 6 TO 8
Vegetable oil for frying, plus 2 tablespoons
1 medium cauliflower, trimmed and cut into florets
2 medium red onions, chopped
One 1-inch fresh ginger, finely chopped
4 cloves garlic, finely chopped
3 dried red chilies, broken
1 bay leaf
3 medium tomatoes, finely chopped
½ cup orange juice
2 teaspoons garam masala
Salt to taste
¼ cup pea shoot leaves

Heat the oil to 350°F and fry the cauliflower florets until lightly golden brown and cooked through. Cautiously remove them, using kitchen tongs or a slotted spoon. Drain the excess oil onto a paper towel.

In a medium pan, heat 2 tablespoons of oil on medium heat and add the onions, ginger, garlic, chilies, and bay leaves. Cook until the onions begin to caramelize, about 5 to 7 minutes. Add a tablespoon of water to prevent the spices from burning.

Add the tomatoes, orange juice, garam masala, salt, and ½ cup water and bring the mixture to a boil. Reduce the heat to low and simmer until the sauce becomes thick and all the flavors are well combined.

Pour the spice mixture over the cauliflower and serve hot, garnished with the pea shoot leaves.

GODDESSES OF FERTILITY OF THE SOIL

I have always been drawn to ancient Indian, Greek, Egyptian, Roman, and many other mythologies. Each of these cultures created beautiful symbols of nature and fertility.

Every form of nature is represented by mythological figures of gods and goddesses. In Egyptian mythology, Sopdet is the goddess of the fertility of the soil and is personified by the "dog star" Sirius. This star was considered the most important of all the stars in the ancient civilization because it came at the time of inundation and the start of the Egyptian New Year. As a goddess of the inundation, she was a goddess of fertility.

In Indian mythology, Annapurna is the goddess of food and nourishment and she brings abundance and prosperity to Earth. Her name itself signifies divine nourishment where *Anna* means food and *Purna* means complete. My beloved principal Parvadha Vardhini Gopalakrishnan gave me an idol of Goddess Annapurna once, and I have kept it in my kitchen since, covered with rice. The principal told me that this signifies abundance.

In Gallo-Roman religion, Rosmerta was the goddess of fertility and abundance, her attributes being those of plenty such as the cornucopia. In Roman mythology cornucopia is the horn of plenty—the symbol of abundance and nourishment. In Hindu mythology, there are fascinating references to *Akshaya Patra*— the magic bowl that is always filled with food and automatically replenishes when some of it is consumed.

Roasted Coconut and Sorrel Leaves

Bright fresh green sorrel leaves bring a nice, tart lemony flavor to this dish. Sorrel has the texture of spinach when cooked, and the flavor is highlighted with the sweet-and-sour tangy kokum. Add sorrel toward the end of the cooking process to minimize the loss of flavor. Roasting coconut makes it rich yet nuttier and adds more depth to the dish.

SERVES 4
2 teaspoons coriander seeds
5 dried red chilies
1 teaspoon peppercorns
4 tablespoons clarified butter
½ cup freshly grated coconut
1 red onion, thinly sliced
1 teaspoon mustard seeds
8 to 10 curry leaves
1 teaspoon turmeric
6 to 8 dried kokum, soaked in ½ cup hot water
1 cup coconut milk
2 pounds fresh sorrel leaves, washed and dried

Dry roast the coriander, chilies, and peppercorns in a small heavy-bottom skillet on medium heat, stirring continuously to ensure even cooking. Remove from the heat and let cool at room temperature. Finely grind the mixture in a coffee or spice grinder and reserve.

Heat 2 tablespoons of clarified butter in a medium saucepan on medium heat and fry the coconut and onion until brown, about 5 to 7 minutes.

Transfer to a blender and combine with ¼ cup of water and grind to a coarse paste.

Heat the remaining clarified butter on medium heat in a saucepan. Add the mustard seeds and curry leaves and fry for a minute. Add the coconut-onion paste and the spice blend with turmeric. Stir well to mix all the flavors.

Add the kokum to the coconut milk and salt and continue to cook until the flavors are well combined, about 3 to 4 minutes. Stir in the sorrel leaves and cook for 2 minutes, until wilted.

Serve hot with boiled rice.

Lime Potatoes Roasted with Spice Blend

These simple, savory, and extremely flavorful crispy potatoes are an instant delight. They are roasted to perfection, infused with the flavors of zesty lemon, warm aromatic spices, and a hint of garlic, and are absolutely one of my favorite dishes.

SERVES 4
1 teaspoon turmeric powder
1 teaspoon cumin powder
1 teaspoon coriander powder
1 teaspoon cayenne pepper
1 teaspoon sugar
1 teaspoon ground black pepper
Juice of 1 lime
4 tablespoons clarified butter
Salt to taste
4 medium potatoes, peeled and halved or quartered, if large
4 cloves garlic, thinly sliced
¼ cup sour cream
Few sprigs fresh mint

Preheat the oven to 400°F.

In a medium mixing bowl, combine turmeric, cumin, coriander, cayenne, sugar, pepper, lime juice, clarified butter, and salt and mix well to make a smooth paste. Add the potatoes, garlic, and sour cream and evenly coat the potatoes with the mixture.

Place the potatoes on a baking dish or a roasting pan and bake until cooked through, about 30 to 40 minutes.

Serve hot, with the mint leaves.

Poppy Seed-Crusted Baby Potatoes

I enjoy cooking with baby potatoes—they are sweeter with a creamier texture than more mature potatoes. Poppy seeds add a nice nutty flavor and crunch, while mango powder adds a wonderful sour tartness. This recipe also tastes great with sesame seeds in place of poppy seeds.

SERVES 4
Vegetable oil for frying, plus 2 tablespoons
1 pound small potatoes (about 1¾-inch diameter), scrubbed
5 tablespoons poppy seeds
2 tablespoons chili flakes
1 teaspoon dried mango powder
½ teaspoon sugar
1 tablespoon tamarind paste
Salt to taste
1 small tomato, seeded and diced
Thyme sprigs

Heat the frying oil to 350°F.

Fry the potatoes until lightly browned, then remove them with a slotted spoon and drain the excess oil onto a paper towel.

In a medium pan, heat 2 tablespoons of oil on medium heat. Add the poppy seeds and cook, stirring continuously until darker in shade and very fragrant, about 2 to 3 minutes.

Add the potatoes, chili flakes, mango powder, sugar, tamarind, and salt and stir to evenly coat the potatoes.

Serve hot, garnished with tomato and thyme.

Spiced Mashed Jaggery Turnips

Come winter a variety of dishes with sweet turnips find their way to our family table. In this recipe, their sweet, sharp taste is enhanced with the natural sweetness of jaggery. This flavorsome hearty dish is a good alternative to mashed potatoes and has more texture and bite. I sometimes roast the turnips before mashing, as it intensifies the sweetness and makes them very tender.

SERVES 4
3 tablespoons vegetable oil
1 red onion, sliced
2 cloves garlic, chopped
1 teaspoon cumin seeds
1 bay leaf
2 medium tomatoes, quartered
1 pound turnips, boiled, peeled, and mashed
Salt to taste
2 tablespoons grated jaggery or brown sugar
2 green chilies, slit in half

Heat the oil in a medium pan over medium heat and fry the onions, garlic, cumin, and bay leaf, stirring continuously until the onions begin to caramelize, about 5 minutes.

Add the tomatoes and cook, stirring until they become mushy and the mixture becomes dry, about 4 to 5 minutes.

Stir in the mashed turnips, salt, jaggery, and chilies and cook until all the flavors are well combined.

Serve hot.

Split Beans and Yam Poriyal

Poriyal, in Tamil, refers to a simple stir-fry vegetable dish with spices and shredded coconut. This easy and healthy recipe can be made using any combination of vegetables. In this dish, split beans and yams combine with some essentials of the South Indian kitchen like mustard seeds, coconut, asafoetida, and curry leaves, which bring in the exotic flavors and aromas that are characteristic of the region.

SERVES 4 TO 6
2 tablespoons coconut or vegetable oil
1 teaspoon mustard seeds
1 teaspoon split black beans
1 dried red chili, halved
½ teaspoon asafoetida
4 to 6 curry leaves
1 pound yams, boiled, peeled, and cut into 1-inch pieces
Salt to taste
⅓ cup freshly grated coconut

Heat the oil and fry the mustard seeds, split beans, chili, asafoetida, and curry leaves until the seeds start crackling and the beans turn darker in color, about 1 to 2 minutes.

Add the yams and salt and stir well to evenly coat with the spice infusion. Stir in the coconut and cook until all the flavors are well combined, about 3 minutes.

Serve hot.

Thai Eggplants in Ginger-Cashew Curry

Sweet and creamy eggplant is simmered with tender melt-in-the-mouth plantains in a rich and delicious cashew curry spiced with ginger. Thai eggplants are generally small and round, and they can be found in a variety of colors—green, white, and purple.

SERVES 4
1 cup raw cashews
3 tablespoons vegetable oil
1 red onion, finely chopped
2 cloves garlic, chopped
One 2-inch fresh ginger, peeled and finely chopped
1 green chili, such as serrano, finely chopped
1 pound Thai eggplants, stemmed
2 plantains, sliced
1 tomato, finely chopped
Salt to taste
10 to 12 fresh basil leaves

Heat a heavy-bottom skillet on medium heat and dry roast the cashews until fragrant and darker in color. Remove from the heat and purée them with ¼ cup of water into a fine paste.

Heat the oil and fry the onions, garlic, ginger, and chili until the onions begin to caramelize, about 7 to 8 minutes.

Stir in the Thai eggplants, plantains, tomato, and salt and fry for 1 minute. Add 1 cup of water with the cashew paste and bring to a boil. Reduce the heat and simmer until the vegetables are cooked and the sauce is thick. Add a little more water if required.

Serve hot, garnished with the basil leaves.

Spiced Paneer with Cinnamon

Paneer is an all-time favorite with vegetarians—versatile and a good substitute for meats in recipes. Complementing the green peas in this dish is paneer is spiced with warm cinnamon and the earthy flavor of aromatic bay leaves.

SERVES 4
2 tablespoons clarified butter
12 ounces fresh paneer, cubed
1 red onion, diced
One 2-inch cinnamon stick
2 bay leaves
1 cup frozen peas, thawed
Salt to taste
1 teaspoon garam masala
Fresh cilantro leaves for garnish

Heat the clarified butter and evenly sear the paneer in batches until golden brown. Remove from the pan and drain the excess oil onto a paper towel.

To the same pan, add the onion, cinnamon, and bay leaves and cook, stirring continuously until the onions soften, about 3 to 4 minutes.

Add the peas and seared paneer and stir well. Add the salt and ¼ cup of water and bring it to boil. Reduce the heat and simmer until all the flavors are well combined.

Season with the garam masala and serve hot, sprinkled with cilantro.

Sautéed Broccoli with Grapefruit

A refreshing recipe using grapefruit juice to liven up the flavors of broccoli. Sautéing broccoli helps retain its color and taste as well as its nutrients, making this a quick, healthy dish. Whole star anise and grapefruit segments help add to the presentation.

SERVES 4
2 tablespoons vegetable oil
3 small shallots, thinly sliced
2 whole star anise
2 broccoli heads, cut into florets
Salt to taste
Freshly ground black pepper to taste
Juice of 1 grapefruit and segments of 1 grapefruit for garnish
Zest of ½ lemon

Heat the oil in a large skillet over medium high heat. Add the shallots and star anise and cook, stirring frequently, until translucent, about 2 minutes.

Add broccoli and season it with salt and pepper and stir. Add the grapefruit juice and reduce the heat to low. Simmer until the juice is almost dried.

Stir in the segments with the lemon zest and serve hot.

IT'S IN THE SOIL

So much has been said about them since the Vedic times—spices, the delicate gifts of nature at its best, are perfumed by Mother Nature herself. One thing that has always intrigued me is not their beauty and fragrance, but their journey. Beginning with the phenomenon of pollination to the blossoms; from farming to curing to drying and…everything that creates them.

As a child, I once took a pod of mustard seeds and pressed it between my fingers. The oil, the aroma, and the texture was amazing.

Every time I see a blossom fallen to the ground, I get mad at gravity. When they are disturbed by birds, I get upset with the glorious chirping sounds in my garden.

I always wondered how the spices were naturally infused with the mystical aromas. As a child, I figured that all these aromas were hiding in the soil and nature injects them into the blossoms.

Radicchio with Sweet Snap Peas

Snap peas have a sweet flavor and great crispy texture. They should be cooked briefly in order to retain that texture. Adding sourness with vinegar and orange juice balances the bitter taste of the pretty, white-veined red leaves of radicchio.

SERVES 4
2 tablespoons olive oil
3 cloves garlic, minced
One 2-inch fresh ginger, peeled and minced
1 green chili, such as serrano or Thai, minced
8 to 10 raw cashews
2 tablespoons cider vinegar
⅓ cup orange juice
1 teaspoon brown sugar
Salt to taste
⅛ teaspoon freshly ground black pepper
½ pound sugar snap peas, ends trimmed
1 head radicchio, very thinly sliced

In a medium saucepan, heat the oil on medium heat. Add the garlic, ginger, chili, and cashews and cook, stirring continuously until fragrant, about 2 minutes. Add the vinegar, orange juice, sugar, salt, and pepper and bring to a boil. Reduce the heat to low and simmer until the liquid is reduced to half. Add the snap peas and toss to evenly coat them.

Remove from heat. Gently toss them with the radicchio and serve immediately.

Tofu with Collards and Fresh Turmeric

In the southern parts of the United States, greens are an essential part of the cuisine. Southerners traditionally serve collard greens on New Year's Day, as they believe that it brings good luck for the coming year. These leafy greens are nutritious—a good source of vitamins. They hold up well to heat and retain their texture. Tofu pairs well with collards and absorbs the flavors of the spices and other ingredients very well.

SERVES 4
1 tablespoon sesame oil
2 garlic cloves, minced
1 red onion, finely chopped
4 to 6 ounces fresh turmeric root, peeled and sliced
One 2-inch fresh ginger, peeled and julienned
3 collard green leaves, stems removed and coarsely chopped
8 to 10 ounces firm tofu, drained and diced into 1-inch pieces
Salt to taste
8 fresh chives, cut into 2-inch pieces

Heat the oil in a large skillet over medium heat. Add the garlic, onion, turmeric root, and ginger and cook until the onions become soft, about 3 to 4 minutes.

Stir in collard greens and cook until evenly coated. Add a tablespoon of water, if required.

Add tofu and salt and cook, stirring until heated through, about 2 minutes.

Season with the chives and serve hot.

Asparagus with Bengal Spice Mix

Asparagus is a healthy addition to any meal and has been considered a delicacy since time immemorial. Elegant stalks of fresh green and succulent asparagus are dressed with the wonderful aromas and flavors of mustard, fennel, cumin, and fenugreek. The woody ends of the asparagus will have to be removed before cooking—easily done by snapping them off with your fingers.

SERVES 4
1 pound tender asparagus, trimmed
4 tablespoons vegetable oil
¼ teaspoon fenugreek seeds
¼ teaspoon cumin seeds
¼ teaspoon fennel seeds
¼ teaspoon mustard seeds
¼ teaspoon onion seeds
Pinch of chili powder
1 medium red onion, sliced
Salt to taste
2 tablespoons lemon juice
½ teaspoon paprika

Fill a large pot with 1 inch of water and bring to a boil. Add the asparagus, cover, and cook until tender-crisp, about 3 to 4 minutes. Drain and reserve.

Heat the oil and fry the fenugreek, cumin, fennel, mustard, onion seeds, and chili powder for 30 seconds. Add the onions and cook until soft, about 2 minutes. Add the asparagus and salt and stir fry for 1 minute, until all flavors are well combined.

Stir in the lemon juice and paprika and serve hot.

Pomegranate-Mint Eggplant

Eggplant belongs to the family of nightshade plants, which grow in shady areas or flower at night. Some people have a sensitivity toward these nightshade vegetables, but in spite of their notoriety, they make some of the most delicious recipes. Purple-skinned glossy eggplant is extremely versatile. The sturdy slices can be roasted or grilled or even lightly fried, as in this recipe. It tastes equally good if baked.

SERVES 4
1 pound Japanese eggplants, trimmed and cut into ½-inch roundels
Salt to taste
½ cup rice flour
4 tablespoons oil, divided
1 cup coconut milk
½ cup fresh pomegranate seeds
2 teaspoons cumin seeds, roasted and coarsely ground
Sprigs of fresh mint

Sprinkle the eggplant with salt and leave to sweat for 15 to 20 minutes.

Evenly dust them with rice flour.

Heat 2 tablespoons of oil in a nonstick pan on medium-high heat. Cook the eggplant in batches, turning it, until golden on both sides. Remove with a slotted spoon and drain onto a paper towel and keep warm. Wipe the pan with a paper towel before cooking each batch.

In a saucepan over medium heat, combine coconut milk, half pomegranate seeds, roasted cumin, and salt and bring to a boil. Reduce heat and continue to cook until the sauce thickens.

Pour sauce over the cooked eggplant and serve hot, garnished with the mint leaves and reserved pomegranate seeds.

Mixed Vegetable Olan

Olan, a mild spiced curry, is one of the essential dishes in the Sadya or the vegetarian banquet of Kerala, especially during the Onam festival. Served on a banana leaf, along with plain boiled rice, traditionally on the floor and eaten with the right hand, olan is one of the main curries served. The feast usually has more than ten dishes in the main course itself. Coconut is an essential ingredient in the Sadya dishes, which are cooked in coconut oil. Olan is usually made with white gourd and cowpeas. In my version of olan, plantains, white squash, carrots, and peas are cooked with the coconut milk.

SERVES 6
2 tablespoons coconut oil
1 teaspoon mustard seeds
One 2-inch fresh ginger, peeled and minced
1 green chili, split
1 can (15.5 ounces) black-eyed peas
2 medium plantains, peeled and sliced
1 white squash, peeled and diced
2 small carrots, peeled and cut into 1-inch dices
½ cup frozen peas, thawed
Salt to taste
½ cup coconut milk
½ cup yogurt, whisked until smooth
2 tablespoons fresh cilantro leaves

Heat the coconut oil in a saucepan over medium heat. Add mustard seeds, ginger, and green chilies and cook until fragrant, about 2 minutes. Add the black-eyed peas, plantains, squash, carrots, and peas and cook, stirring until well coated with the spices. Add salt, coconut milk, and yogurt and bring to a boil. Reduce the heat and simmer until the vegetables are cooked through and the sauce is thick.

Serve hot, garnished with the cilantro.

Carrots and Green Beans with Lemongrass

A quick and simple dish, carrots and green beans—two very healthy vegetables—are paired with the refreshing citrus flavors of lemongrass and tinged with spicy ginger.

I like adding lemongrass at the beginning along with other spices, as it adds a strong lemony taste and aroma, as compared to a mild flavor when added toward the end.

SERVES 4 TO 6
2 tablespoons oil
1 teaspoon cumin seeds
Pinch of asafoetida
One 2-inch fresh ginger, peeled and julienned
1 stalk lemongrass, finely chopped
½ cup heavy cream
6 carrots, peeled and sliced into long strips
8 to 10 ounces tender green beans
Salt to taste
Juice of 1 lemon

Heat oil in a skillet over medium heat. Add cumin seeds, asafoetida, ginger, and lemongrass and cook until very fragrant, about 1 to 2 minutes. Add 1 tablespoon of water to prevent burning the spices, if required. Stir in the cream, carrots, green beans, and salt and cook until vegetables are crisp-tender, about 5 to 6 minutes.

Add the lemon juice and serve hot.

Crunchy Snap Peas and Pearl Onions

Sweet, crunchy snap peas get an Asian burst of flavor when sautéed with soy sauce and scallions and a nice zesty kick from the red chili flakes. I love the sweet mild flavor of whole red pearl onions. Their small size and color complements the bright-green fresh snap peas and adds to the presentational appeal of the dish. I always add snap peas toward the end of the cooking process to help them retain their crunchiness.

SERVES 4 TO 6
2 tablespoons sesame oil
4 cloves garlic, sliced
2 scallions, finely chopped
1 tablespoon red chili flakes
1 teaspoon soy sauce
8 to 10 ounces snap peas, trimmed
8 to 10 baby carrots, trimmed and peeled
4 ounces red pearl onions
Salt to taste

Heat the sesame oil in a wok over medium heat. Add the garlic, scallions, red chili, and soy sauce and cook for 1 minute until the flavors are well combined. Reduce the heat and add the snap peas, carrots, onions, and salt. Stir and cook covered, about 2 to 3 minutes. Add 1 tablespoon of water if required.

Serve hot.

Mushrooms with Mint and Mango Powder

In this easy and delicious recipe, fresh mint and tart mango powder, along with fragrant Madras curry powder, create a perfect balance of spicy, sour, and warm flavors.

Soft earthy mushrooms are a great combination with refreshing mint and make a great side dish for any meal. Sometimes, I also like to combine different varieties of mushrooms to create great textures and color.

SERVES 4
2 tablespoons clarified butter
1 pound fresh button mushrooms, sliced lengthwise
6 to 8 shallots, peeled and cut into halves
3 cloves garlic, minced
2 teaspoons Madras curry powder
Salt to taste
¼ cup fresh mint leaves
1 teaspoon mango powder

Heat the clarified butter over medium heat in a skillet with a tight lid. Add the mushrooms, shallots, garlic, Madras curry powder, and salt. Cover and cook until the mushrooms are cooked through, about 5 minutes. Add 1 tablespoon of water if required.

Serve hot, garnished with the mint leaves and mango powder.

RICE

Kerala Red Rice with Spinach and Nutmeg

Robust and earthy Kerala red rice is spiced with the warm and intense flavors of freshly grated nutmeg. Grown in the Palakkad area of Kerala, this rice is popular in that region for its rich and refreshingly unique taste. It combines wonderfully with the vibrant green spinach. I like pairing fresh fruits with this rice.

SERVES 4

1 cup Kerala red rice, washed and soaked for 1 hour
3 cups vegetable stock
Salt to taste
2 tablespoons vegetable oil
4 cloves garlic, cut into slivers
1 green chili, finely chopped
1 teaspoon crushed coriander seeds
2-inch stick cinnamon
1 large tomato, finely chopped
8 ounces baby spinach, washed, patted dry, and coarsely chopped
¼ teaspoon grated nutmeg

Drain the soaked rice and combine with the vegetable stock and salt in a large saucepan. Place the pan over medium-high heat and cook, stirring occasionally until the rice is cooked but retains a bite, about 20 to 25 minutes. Remove from flame, drain, and set aside.

Heat the oil in a large frying pan over medium heat, add garlic, and sauté until golden. Remove some of the sautéed garlic for garnish and keep aside. Add the chili, coriander seeds, and cinnamon to the pan with tomato and cook until the tomato is mushy, 4 to 5 minutes. Add the spinach and nutmeg and when spinach just wilts, toss in the rice.

Serve hot, garnished with the sautéed garlic.

Roasted Eggplant and Basil Pilaf

Tossing the smoky, caramelized eggplant in a rice pilaf is an interesting way to bring variation to a regular vegetable pilaf. Balsamic vinegar adds a deep tanginess, which complements the natural flavors of the eggplant. The roasting can be done in advance for convenience. Basil is added right toward the end of the cooking to retain maximum flavor and aroma.

SERVES 4
1 large eggplant, cut into 1-inch cubes
2 tablespoons olive oil
1 tablespoon balsamic vinegar
½ teaspoon dried oregano
½ teaspoon red chili flakes
Salt to taste
Freshly ground black pepper to taste
1 cup basmati or any long grain rice, washed and drained
⅓ cup fresh basil leaves

Preheat oven to 300°F.

In a mixing bowl, combine the eggplant with 1 tablespoon of the olive oil, balsamic vinegar, oregano, chili flakes, salt, and pepper. Toss well and spread out on a baking tray lined with foil. Roast in the preheated oven for 10 to 12 minutes. When done, remove from the oven and set aside.

Meanwhile, combine rice with 3 cups of water and salt in a saucepan and boil over medium-high heat until the rice is tender but retains a bite, about 15 minutes. Drain the rice when done.

Heat the remaining olive oil in a large frying pan, add the roasted eggplant and boiled rice, and toss well.

Add the basil, toss well, and serve hot.

Split Gram and Peas Pilaf

Split grams offer a nice nutty taste while the peas add a subtle sweetness to this easy and popular rice pilaf. Rich and aromatic cloves, cardamom, and bay leaves add layers of flavors. The warm, enticing aroma makes it a simple and quick side dish to go with curries or even just raita.

SERVES 4
2 tablespoons vegetable oil
1 large bay leaf
3 cloves
3 pods cardamom
One 3-inch cinnamon stick
1 medium onion, thinly sliced
⅓ cup split gram, rinsed and drained
1 cup basmati rice, rinsed and drained
2½ cups vegetable stock or water
Salt to taste
Freshly ground pepper to taste
⅓ cup frozen peas, thawed

Heat the oil in a large saucepan over medium heat. Add the bay leaf, cardamom, and cinnamon and cook for 1 minute. When the spices become fragrant, add onion and sauté until soft, about 2 to 3 minutes. Add the split gram to the mixture and continue to cook for 2 minutes. Stir in the rice and sauté the mixture well for about 2 minutes, then stir in the stock or water with salt and pepper. Cook the mixture, stirring occasionally until half the moisture is absorbed.

Mix in the peas and continue cooking until all the moisture is absorbed and the rice and gram are tender but retain a bite.

Serve hot.

Roasted Apple and Kokum Rice

Slow cooking intensifies the sweet flavors and adds a nice chewy texture to the apple wedges. I like to use kokum as a substitute for tamarind in recipes to add sourness and an earthy flavor. More so because the flavors are reminiscent of some very memorable Konkani meals I had in Mangalore. I remember large kokum trees and ripe fruits that we picked, dried, and used for making a cooling summer drink.

SERVES 4
2 red apples, cored and cut into wedges
2 tablespoons olive oil
Juice of 1 large lemon
½ teaspoon dried mint
1 teaspoon red chili flakes
Salt to taste
1 cup basmati rice, rinsed and drained
4 petals dried kokum, cut into strips
¼ teaspoon sugar
1 tablespoon thyme leaves

Preheat the oven to 300°F.

In a mixing bowl, combine the apples with 1 tablespoon olive oil, lemon juice, dried mint, chili flakes, and salt. Toss well and spread over a baking tray lined with foil. Roast in the preheated oven for 8 to 10 minutes. Remove when done.

Meanwhile combine the rice with 2 cups of hot water and salt in a saucepan and cook over medium-low heat. Stir occasionally and cook until all the moisture is absorbed and the rice is tender. Remove from flame and fluff the rice with a fork.

Heat the remaining olive oil in a large frying pan over medium heat. Add the roasted apples, kokum, and sugar and sauté for a minute. Add the cooked rice and toss very well.

Serve hot, garnished with the thyme.

Moilee Rice

Moilee is a popular Kerala curry generally made with seafood. In this vegetarian version, I have added the rich sauce to the rice to make a memorable creamy dish full of spicy coconut flavor and the aroma of curry leaves characteristic of the beautiful coastal region.

SERVES 4
1 cup short grain rice, washed and soaked for 20 minutes
Salt to taste
2 tablespoons coconut oil
1 medium sprig, fresh curry leaves
1 teaspoon black mustard seeds
1 medium onion, finely sliced
2 green chilies, slit lengthwise
One 2-inch fresh ginger, peeled and grated
½ teaspoon ground turmeric
½ cup coconut milk
3 to 4 pieces dried coconut

Combine the rice with 2 cups of water and salt in a saucepan and bring to a boil over medium heat. Cook until all the moisture is absorbed and the rice is tender. Remove from flame and fluff the rice with a fork.

Heat the coconut oil in a large frying pan over medium heat. Add the curry leaves and when crisp, remove from the pan and reserve for garnish. Add the mustard seeds to the same oil. When the mustard crackles, add the onion, chilies, ginger, and turmeric and sauté until onions are translucent. Stir in the coconut milk and when sauce thickens toss in cooked rice.

Serve hot, garnished with the fried curry leaves and dried coconut.

Tamarind Leaf Curd Rice

Yogurt rice is a simple comfort food made delicious with a tempering of mustard seeds and curry leaves. Tamarind leaves add a nice sour flavor to the recipe. This dish tastes even better when served with a pickle of your choice.

SERVES 4
1 cup short grain rice, washed and soaked for 20 minutes
Salt to taste
3 cups plain yogurt, whisked until smooth
½ cup whole milk
1 tablespoon clarified butter
¼ teaspoon asafoetida
1 teaspoon mustard seeds
1 teaspoon cumin seeds
8 to 10 fresh curry leaves
1 sprig fresh tamarind leaves
3 to 4 sambar chilies or dried red chilies

Drain the rice and combine with the salt and 2 cups of water in a saucepan over medium heat. Cook the mixture, stirring occasionally until all the moisture is absorbed and the rice is tender, about 15 minutes. Fluff the rice with a fork and cool slightly.

Combine the cooked rice in a large mixing bowl with the yogurt and milk and mix very well, adding some more salt if required.

Heat the clarified butter in a small frying pan over medium heat and add the remaining ingredients. When the spices crackle and the curry leaves turn crisp, pour the mixture over the rice and mix well.

Serve warm.

Spiced Curry Leaf Pomegranate Rice

This rice gets a bold tanginess from dried pomegranate, a wonderful nuttiness from sesame seeds, and a pungent spiciness from ginger and dried red chilies. Short grain rice is slightly tender and stickier than long grain rice, which works perfectly for this recipe.

SERVES 4
1 cup short grain rice, washed and drained
Salt to taste
2 tablespoons sesame oil
1 teaspoon mustard seeds
2 tablespoons white sesame seeds
10 to 12 fresh curry leaves
4 to 6 sambar chilies or dried red chilies
One 2-inch fresh ginger, peeled and grated
1 tablespoon dried pomegranate seeds, coarsely ground

Drain the rice and combine with the salt and 2 cups of water in a saucepan over medium heat. Cook the mixture, stirring occasionally until all the moisture is absorbed and the rice is tender, about 12 to 15 minutes. Fluff the rice with a fork and set aside.

Heat the sesame oil in a large frying pan over medium-high heat and add the mustard seeds. When the mustard crackles, add sesame seeds, curry leaves, chilies, ginger, and pomegranate seeds and sauté the mixture until the curry leaves are dry and crisp. Toss in the rice and mix until the rice is well coated with all the flavors.

Serve hot.

THE SACRED TULSI

Traditionally, one often finds a tulsi (holy basil) plant at the entrance of Hindu households. They say tulsi protects the family from the evil eye and also brings good luck. We had tulsi in the center of the courtyard, but later it was moved to the side because our new car, a Maruti 800, had to be parked in that space! Though it was moved to the side, it still remained at the center of the morning rituals. Biji would gently water the tulsi with the holy water from Ganges that she kept in her temple at home, along with her morning prayers. She would pluck a few leaves, add it to glass of charnamrit or divine nectar.

We would be given the holy water and the sacred ritual was to accept it in a cup or in the well of the right palm with the left hand lightly under it.

After drinking it, I would wipe my wet palm over my head because it was for wisdom, according to Biji. My day would be made when I would get one leaf in my charnamrit. I always relished the refreshing taste.

The soil in which Tulsi grows is considered very sacred too. Even the dried leaves and the twigs. Sometimes when we went on a long uncertain journey, a little soil was rubbed on our forehead for protection. It would feel cool against my skin, but I would feel protected.

I remember going to Haridwar with my grandparents, and we brought back a little soil from the banks of the Ganges and that was added to the tulsi pot in our house.

It is believed that when a newlywed bride enters her in-laws' house, she brings a little soil from her parents house which is added to the tulsi plant in her new home. I think it must be symbolic of creating oneness between the two families.

Hibiscus and Green Mango Rice

A simple rice dish in which hibiscus imparts a purple-crimson color and tangy floral flavor. Dried hibiscus petals, also known as *flor de Jamaica* in Spanish, is a popular ingredient in Mexico and is used for making refreshing teas, cooling drinks, and even sauces. Green mango adds a beautiful layer of sourness and texture to the rice.

SERVES 6
¼ cup dried hibiscus petals
2 tablespoons butter
4 green cardamom pods
4 cloves
1 cup basmati rice, soaked for 30 minutes and drained
Salt to taste
1 green mango, sliced
1 teaspoon red chili flakes
Freshly ground black pepper to taste

Combine the hibiscus with 2 cups of water in a saucepan and bring to a boil over high heat. Boil the mixture for 3 to 4 minutes, remove from the flame, cover, and set aside.

Heat 1 tablespoon of butter in a large saucepan over medium heat. Add the cardamom and cloves and when they sizzle, add the rice and salt. Sauté for 3 to 4 minutes. Strain in the hibiscus water and cook, stirring occasionally until all the moisture is absorbed and the rice is tender, about 8 to 10 minutes. When done, remove from the flame and fluff the rice with a fork. Heat the remaining butter in a large frying pan, add the mango and chili flakes, and sauté for 1 minute.

Add rice and toss well. Serve hot.

Minty Mushroom and Barley Pilaf

A new and interesting side dish made with pearl barley, a nutritious grain with a chewy texture and nutty flavor. Another interesting ingredient is pippali peppers, and I treasure them the most because of their characteristic aroma and pungent taste. It is a key ingredient for Ayurveda rasayana to promote rejuvenation and longevity.

SERVES 4
2 tablespoons butter
3 cloves garlic, finely sliced
1 medium onion, finely chopped
1 cup sliced button mushrooms
1 teaspoon crushed pippali peppercorns
Salt to taste
Freshly ground black pepper to taste
1½ cups pearl barley
2 fresh red chilies, sliced
¼ cup fresh mint leaves, chopped

Heat the butter in a large saucepan over medium heat, add garlic and onion, and sauté until onions are translucent. Add the mushrooms, pippali, salt, pepper, and barley and sauté until the mushrooms begin to dry, about 3 to 4 minutes.

Stir in 3½ to 4 cups of hot water. Cook the mixture stirring occasionally until the barley is cooked. Keep mixing in more stock or water if required, about 20 to 25 minutes.

Mix in the mint leaves, remove from heat, and serve hot.

Vermicelli Pilaf with French Beans and Ginger

Vermicelli has been used in pilafs for a long time. In Middle Eastern countries like Egypt, Armenia, and even Turkey, the vermicelli is lightly toasted in butter to make it golden brown before adding it to the recipe. In this dish, vermicelli is the main ingredient along with French beans and apricots, and it makes a wonderful one-pot meal. You can use any kind of vermicelli to make this dish.

SERVES 4
2 tablespoons clarified butter
One 2-inch fresh ginger, peeled and julienned
1 small onion, finely chopped
2 teaspoons curry powder
6 to 8 ounces French beans, chopped and blanched
5 to 6 dried apricots, cut in half
8 ounces vermicelli
1 medium tomato, seeded and thinly sliced
Salt to taste
10 to 12 green olives
¼ cup fresh parsley leaves, chopped

Heat the clarified butter in a heavy-bottom pan over medium heat. Add the ginger and onion and sauté until the onion softens. Add the curry powder, French beans, apricots, and vermicelli and sauté gently for 3 to 5 minutes, taking care not to crush the vermicelli. Stir in ½ cup boiling water, the tomato, and the salt and cook until vermicelli is tender and the mixture is dry.

Stir in the olives and parsley and serve hot.

Wheat Berry Pilaf with Edamame

Edamame make a great addition to salads and pilafs and taste great eaten steamed and salted right out of the pod. An important part of Chinese and Japanese cuisine, edamame are green soybeans and are high in protein. The flavors of the pilaf come together with edamame, smoky paprika, and licorice-like star anise. Wheat berry gives this dish a nice earthy, chewy texture.

SERVES 4
1 cup wheat berries
Salt to taste
3 teaspoons olive oil
3 whole star anise
1 large onion, finely chopped
1 cup edamame, thawed if frozen
1 teaspoon hot smoked paprika
Freshly ground black pepper to taste
½ cup grated parmesan
2 to 3 fresh red chilies
Sprigs of fresh cilantro

Combine the wheat berries with 4 cups of water and the salt in a large saucepan and bring to a boil over medium-high heat. Cook, stirring occasionally until the berries are plump and tender, about 35 to 40 minutes. Drain away the extra moisture, fluff with a fork, and set aside.

Heat the oil in a large frying pan, add star anise and onion and sauté until the onion is golden. Add edamame, paprika, and pepper and sauté for 2 to 3 minutes. Toss in the cooked wheat berries and parmesan and cook until mixture is slightly creamy.

Serve hot, with red chili and cilantro.

Pumpkin Biryani with Pistachios

A quick and easy biryani recipe made with quinoa. This healthy gluten-free cereal cooks fast and has a chewy yet fluffy texture. It is a good substitute for rice or even couscous.

It is important to rinse the quinoa very well before cooking to remove the natural coating, which has a slightly bitter taste.

SERVES 4

2 tablespoons olive oil
1 teaspoon fennel seeds
1 onion, finely chopped
2 garlic cloves, crushed
1 pound pumpkin, peeled, seeded, and cut into ¾-inch cubes
1 teaspoon cayenne pepper
1½ cups quinoa, well rinsed and drained
½ cup pistachios, shelled
Salt to taste
Freshly ground black pepper to taste
⅛ teaspoon grated nutmeg
¼ cup fresh parsley leaves

Heat the oil in a large saucepan over medium heat. Add the fennel, onion, and garlic and sauté until the onions are golden. Add the pumpkin, cayenne pepper, and quinoa with half the pistachios and sauté for 4 to 5 minutes. Stir in 3 cups of hot water with the salt, pepper, and nutmeg. Cook, stirring occasionally until the quinoa is tender, the pumpkin is cooked, and all the moisture is absorbed.

Serve hot, garnished with remaining pistachios and parsley.

Roasted Cauliflower Pilaf with Olives

Tender pieces of roasted, garlicky cauliflower with spiced onions and sweet pimento-stuffed olives. The rice cooked in vegetable broth gives the pilaf more flavor. Served with yogurt and pickle, this makes for a complete comfort meal.

SERVES 4
1 pound cauliflower, separated into florets
4 tablespoons olive oil
5 garlic cloves, crushed
¼ teaspoon ground fenugreek seeds
Salt to taste
2 onions, finely chopped
1 teaspoon chili powder
½ teaspoon ground turmeric
12 to 15 pimento-stuffed olives, plus extra for garnish
1 cup arborio or any other round grain rice
Freshly ground black pepper to taste
2 scallions, trimmed and finely chopped
2 fresh red chilies, coarsely chopped
2 lemons, cut into wedges

Preheat oven to 300°F.

In a mixing bowl, combine the cauliflower with 1 tablespoon of olive oil, half the garlic, ground fenugreek, and salt and toss well. Spread the cauliflower on a baking tray lined with foil and roast in the preheated oven for 7 to 8 minutes.

Heat the remaining olive oil in a large frying pan over medium heat. Add remaining garlic and sauté until fragrant. Add onions, chili powder, turmeric, olives, and rice and sauté until the mixture is very fragrant, about 2 to 3 minutes.

Stir in about 3 cups of hot water, salt, and pepper and cook stirring, occasionally until the rice is tender. Mix more water if required. When rice is cooked through and all moisture has been absorbed, toss in the roasted cauliflower, remove from heat, and serve hot with lemon wedges.

BREADS

Buckwheat Shallot Crêpes

Crêpes are infinitely adaptable—sweet or savory—and are great any time of the day. These crispy buckwheat crêpes are healthy and gluten-free, with an earthy and nutty flavor. Letting the batter ferment overnight will result in delicious, light, and airy crêpes. The filling as well as the crêpes can be made in advance and reheated right before serving.

SERVES 4
About ¾ cup whole milk
2 tablespoons clarified butter
1 cup buckwheat flour
Salt to taste
½ teaspoon turmeric
2 tablespoons vegetable oil
4 shallots, thinly sliced
1 teaspoon cumin seeds

Combine the milk, clarified butter, buckwheat flour, salt, and turmeric in a blender and process until the batter is smooth. Pour the batter into a bowl. Cover and leave the batter at room temperature for at least an hour.

Heat ½ tablespoon of oil over medium heat. Swirl the pan to evenly coat the base with the oil.

Scoop ¼ of the batter and pour it onto the pan. Quickly swirl it around with one circular motion to get a very thin and even spread in the pan. Sprinkle it with ¼ of the shallots and a pinch of cumin seeds.

Cook the crêpe for about 1 minute, until the batter begins to bubble and the edges are brown. Slide a metal spatula along the edges to loosen the crêpe and flip it over to the other side. Cook for another minute until the crêpe is browned and crisp on the edges. Repeat the process for the remaining ingredients.

Serve hot.

Apricot and Plum Pancakes

Barley plus whole wheat flour becomes a perfect combination when merged with the rich and aromatic flavors of plum and sweet apricots. Barley flour is an excellent source of fiber and nutrients and gives this breakfast recipe a soft cake-like texture. Generally, one-third to one-half of the flour in a recipe can be substituted with barley flour. If you want, you can dry roast the barley lightly before adding to the pancake mixture as that brings out the sweet nutty flavors of the barley.

SERVES 4 TO 6
1 cup barley flour
1 cup whole wheat flour, plus more for dusting and rolling
1 tablespoon sugar
Salt to taste
2 ripe apricots, pitted and finely chopped
2 ripe plums, pitted and finely chopped
¾ cup whole milk, plus more if required
3 tablespoons unsalted butter

In a large mixing bowl, combine both flours, sugar, and salt. Add apricots and plums and mix well. Add milk, a little at a time, to form a pliable dough. Cover with a damp kitchen towel and let it rest for at least 30 minutes at room temperature.

Divide the dough into 6 equal pieces. Place one piece of the dough on a lightly floured surface and slightly flatten with your palm. Using a lightly floured rolling pin, roll out the dough to a ¼-inch-thick round.

Heat a nonstick griddle over medium heat and lightly grease it. Place the rolled dough on the hot griddle and cook until each side is lightly browned, about 30 seconds on each side.

Remove pancake to a serving plate. Repeat the process with the remaining dough.

South Indian Pancakes with Orange and Roasted Beets

In this variation of the popular and easy South Indian pancake, uttapam, the batter is made using semolina instead of lentils and rice. The toppings of sweet-and-sour tangy oranges and delicious beets add a nice color and presentation to the dish. This recipe tastes great with a topping of just about any vegetable or fruit of your choice.

SERVES 6
1 cup semolina
1 cup plain yogurt, whisked until smooth
Salt to taste
3 tablespoons oil
2 oranges, peeled and segmented
2 medium beets, roasted, peeled, and finely chopped
4 cloves garlic, sliced
1 tablespoon chili flakes
¼ cup fresh mint leaves

Heat a small saucepan over medium-low heat and roast the semolina for 2 minutes, stirring until fragrant.

In a mixing bowl, combine the roasted semolina, yogurt, and salt to make a batter of pancake consistency, adding water if needed. Cover and rest for 15 minutes.

Heat a griddle or nonstick pan on medium heat and grease with a little oil. Lightly whisk the batter and pour a ladleful onto the pan. Spread evenly with the back of the spoon to make a round, 4 to 6 inches in diameter.

Immediately layer it with the orange segments and beets in a symmetrical design. Top with the garlic and chili flakes.

Drizzle some oil over and around the pancake. Continue to cook until cooked through, 1 to 2 minutes. Turn over and cook the other side until golden brown, another minute.

Serve hot garnished with the mint leaves and a chutney of your choice.

Spicy Zucchini Ginger-Chili Pancakes

A quick and simple recipe for savory pancakes. Topped with soft and delicately flavored thin zucchini slices, ginger, and green chilies makes this a delight. The baking powder and buttermilk added to the batter make them extra light and fluffy with a spongy texture.

SERVES 4
1 cup all-purpose flour
1 tablespoon sugar
2 teaspoons baking powder
Salt to taste
1 cup buttermilk
2 tablespoons vegetable oil, plus more if required
1 zucchini, thinly sliced
One 2-inch fresh ginger, peeled and minced
3 chilies, such as serrano, minced

In a medium bowl, whisk together the flour, sugar, baking powder, and salt. Add the buttermilk and whisk to make a smooth batter.

Heat a large nonstick skillet or griddle over medium heat. Brush lightly with oil.

For each pancake, put 2 to 3 tablespoons of batter onto a skillet. Using the back of the spoon, spread batter into a round, 3 inches in diameter. Garnish the pancake with a slice of zucchini, ginger, and chilies.

Drizzle some oil over and around the pancake. Continue to cook until bubbles form on the surface, 1 to 2 minutes. Turn over and cook the other side until golden brown, another minute.

Repeat the process with the remaining batter and serve pancakes hot with any chutney of your choice.

Rustic Salt and Spice Bread

A simple dough made with cumin, coriander, and salt, this crispy bread tastes great fresh off the griddle. Chili flakes and black peppercorns highlight its flavors; chili flakes enhance the overall taste of the other spices, while chili adds a sharp heat to the overall taste of the dish.

MAKES 8
1 cup unbleached all-purpose flour, plus more for rolling and dusting
1 cup barley flour
2 tablespoons clarified butter, plus more for shallow frying
2 teaspoons cumin seeds
1½ teaspoons black peppercorns, lightly crushed
1 tablespoon chili flakes
1 tablespoon coriander seeds, lightly crushed
Salt to taste
¼ cup chopped fresh cilantro

In a medium bowl, combine both the flours, clarified butter, cumin, black peppercorns, chili flakes, coriander seeds, salt, and cilantro with 1 cup of water. Knead to form a soft pliable dough. Cover with a damp kitchen towel and let it rest for at least 30 minutes at room temperature.

Divide dough into 8 equal pieces. Place one piece of the dough on a lightly floured surface and slightly flatten with your palm. Using a lightly floured rolling pin, roll out the dough to a ¼-inch-thick round.

Heat a nonstick griddle over medium heat and lightly grease it. Place the rolled dough on the hot griddle and cook until each side is lightly browned, about 2 minutes on each side.

Remove bread to a serving plate. Repeat the process with the remaining dough.

Savory Corn Bread with Black Cardamom

The smoky flavor of the black cardamom combines well with the juicy and tender corn and fresh cilantro in this flatbread recipe. The classic pairing of spicy ginger and pungent garlic ensures flavors are pleasing to the palate.

MAKES 8
2½ cups whole wheat flour, plus more for rolling and dusting
1 cup fresh corn kernels
Salt to taste
One 1-inch fresh ginger, peeled and minced
3 large cloves garlic, minced
1 teaspoon black cardamom seeds, finely ground
2 to 3 tablespoons, fresh cilantro leaves
6 to 8 tablespoons vegetable oil

In a medium bowl, combine the flour, corn, salt, ginger, garlic, black cardamom, and cilantro with 1 cup of water. Knead to form a soft pliable dough. Add a little extra water, if required. Cover with a damp kitchen towel and let it rest for at least 30 minutes at room temperature.

Divide the dough into 8 equal pieces. Place one piece of the dough on a lightly floured surface and slightly flatten with your palm. Using a lightly floured rolling pin, roll out the dough to a ¼-inch-thick round.

Heat a nonstick griddle over medium heat and lightly grease it. Place the rolled dough on the hot griddle and cook until each side is lightly browned, about 1 to 2 minutes on each side.

Remove bread to a serving plate. Repeat the process with the remaining dough.

Sichuan Pepper Bread

My fascination with the subtle spicy and aromatic Sichuan peppercorns began during my travels to the Himalayan region to learn about its culture and cuisine. The peppercorns' rich red color and lemony, woody flavor are addictive and unforgettable. Dry roasting them before adding to the recipe enhances their flavor while the tongue-tingling sensation is a characteristic of this spice.

MAKES 8 ROUNDS

3 cups all-purpose flour, plus more for rolling and dusting
2 teaspoons baking powder
Salt to taste
½ cup hot milk
1 cup lightly toasted mixed nuts, such as pecans, walnuts, and pistachios, coarsely chopped
2 medium boiled potatoes, peeled and mashed
1 teaspoon Sichuan peppercorns, dry-roasted and finely ground
3 tablespoons sunflower or vegetable oil

Place the flour, baking powder, and salt in a food processor and pulse to mix well. With the motor running, cautiously first pour the hot milk and then 1 to 1½ cups of hot water through the feed tube. Process until the mixture forms a soft pliable ball of dough. Process for 1 minute longer, then turn the dough out onto a lightly floured surface. Knead briefly, cover with plastic wrap, and let it sit for 15 minutes at room temperature.

In a medium bowl, combine the nuts, salt, mashed potatoes, and Sichuan peppercorns. Mix well.

Divide the dough into 8 equal pieces. Working with one piece at a time, roll out the dough onto a lightly floured surface to a circle, 3 to 4 inches in diameter. Brush lightly with oil. Spoon the potato mixture into the center of the round. Gather the edges and bring them together in the center to form a pouch in order to enclose the filling. Press the ends together tightly to close the pouch. Once sealed, press down gently to flatten so that you have a flattened pouch. Roll this pouch into a 7-to-8-inch circle.

Heat a nonstick griddle over medium heat and lightly grease it. Place the rolled dough on the hot griddle and cook until each side is lightly browned, about 1 to 2 minutes on each side.

Remove bread to a serving plate. Repeat the process with the remaining dough.

THE BREAD STORY

Flatbreads were the first breads ever baked. There is something very sacred about the whole ritual. Starting with the dry flour being poured from the container to the mixing bowl, to the ingredients and liquids that vary with cultures and recipes, to rolling it out and cooking it—every part of the process is soul-binding for me.

I always consider making breads a communal activity. As a child, I remember when my Biji would make the dough in the afternoon, wrap it with a damp cloth, and place it in a beige cotton bag to take to the little roadside kiosk and have it cooked on the communal tandoor, also known as "sanjha chula."

We never knew the name of the elderly lady who cooked the breads for us; we only knew her as "Bibi," or Mother. The first thing she did after taking the dough from my hands was throw the first piece into the tandoor as an offering to the fire and soil. And then she would start cooking the breads. On some occasions, such as when guests were coming for dinner, my grandmother would also send along spiced potatoes to be stuffed in the breads as a special treat.

Honey and Sesame Comfort Bread

Gram or chickpea flour or besan has a warm nutty flavor, and is high in protein and gluten free. It is combined with whole wheat flour that binds the dough together and is also a nutritious grain, thus making this bread a tasty and healthy alternative. Toasted sesame seeds add a nice delicate crunch along with the subtle sweetness of honey brushed onto the fresh warm breads, right before serving.

SERVES 4
2 cups whole wheat flour, plus more for rolling and dusting
1 cup gram flour
Salt to taste
3 tablespoons clarified butter
2 tablespoons honey
3 tablespoons white sesame seeds, lightly roasted

In a large mixing bowl, combine both flours and salt and mix well. Add 1¼ cups of water, a little at a time, to form a pliable dough. Cover with a damp kitchen towel and let it rest for at least 30 minutes at room temperature.

Divide the dough into 4 equal pieces. Place one piece of the dough on a lightly floured surface and slightly flatten with your palm. Using a lightly floured rolling pin, roll out the dough to a ¼-inch-thick round.

Heat a nonstick griddle over medium heat and lightly grease it. Place the rolled dough on the hot griddle and cook until each side is lightly browned, about 2 to 3 minutes on each side.

Remove bread to a serving plate. Lightly brush the bread with the honey and sprinkle with the toasted sesame.

Repeat the process with the remaining dough.

Serve hot.

Lama's Tibetan Flatbread

This bread is a souvenir of my trip to Bodhgaya, to meet His Holiness the Dalai Lama and interview him for *The Wheel of Dharma*, my Holy Kitchens film on Buddhism, in which he speaks about peace and the power of food. This bread is traditionally not made with turmeric, but I add it in this recipe because I love its vibrant, yellow color.

SERVES 6

2 cups all-purpose flour, plus more for rolling and dusting
1 teaspoon ground turmeric
1 tablespoon chili flakes
½ teaspoon baking powder
Salt to taste
2 tablespoons yogurt
4 tablespoons clarified butter

In a medium bowl, combine the flour, turmeric, chili flakes, baking powder, salt, and yogurt and mix well. Add about ¾ cup of warm water, a little at a time, to form a smooth pliable dough. Cover with a damp kitchen towel and let it rest for at least 20 minutes at room temperature.

Divide the dough into 6 equal pieces. Place one piece of the dough on a lightly floured surface and slightly flatten with your palm. Using a lightly floured rolling pin, roll out dough into a ¼-inch-thick oval.

Heat a heavy-bottom cast iron skillet over medium heat and lightly grease it with clarified butter. Dock the dough with a fork and transfer it onto the skillet. Place it on the hot griddle. Cover and cook until each side is lightly browned, about 1 minute on each side.

Remove the bread to a serving plate. Repeat the process with the remaining dough.

Serve hot, with the plain yogurt.

Poori Stuffed with Mixed Sprouts

This is a great poori variation made with a stuffing of mixed sprouts, cumin seeds, and garam masala. Sprouts are one of the most nutritious foods, and added to this whole wheat flatbread along with pickle or raita, they make for a wholesome meal.

These pooris remains soft and can be made in advance and lightly reheated in a preheated oven without them becoming hard.

SERVES 4 TO 6
1 cup mixed sprouts
1 teaspoon cumin seeds
1 teaspoon garam masala
Salt to taste
½ teaspoon chili powder
2 cups whole wheat flour, plus more for rolling and dusting
3 tablespoons vegetable oil, plus more for deep frying

In a large mixing bowl, combine the cumin seeds, garam masala, salt, chili powder, and flour and mix well. Add ⅔ cup of warm water, a little at a time, to form a pliable dough. Cover with a damp kitchen towel and let it rest for at least 30 minutes at room temperature.

Divide the dough into 8 equal pieces. Working with one piece at a time, roll out the dough onto a lightly floured surface to a circle, 6 inches in diameter. Brush lightly with oil. Spoon the sprouts into the center of the round. Gather the edges and bring them together in the center to form a pouch to enclose the filling. Press the ends together tightly to close the pouch. Once sealed, press down gently to flatten so that you have a flattened pouch. Roll this pouch into a 4-to-6-inch disc.

Heat the oil in a wok over medium-high heat. Gently add the rolled discs into the hot oil, one at a time, turning once, until golden brown, 3 to 4 minutes. Press each rolled disc gently beneath the surface of the oil with a slotted spoon to ensure it puffs slightly.

Drain onto a paper towel. Repeat the process for the remaining dough.

Jaggery and Cardamom Festive Bread

A variation of the Marathi bread puran poli, this recipe has a mixture of lentils, jaggery, and cardamom as the stuffing, and is flavored with coconut. Jaggery imparts a healthy sweetness and the cardamom a rich citrusy flavor. I like to grind the cardamom right before adding it to the recipe since the flavor is most intense and aromatic when it is freshly ground. Also, lightly toasting the grated coconut before adding it to the flour enhances its sweetness and texture.

SERVES 8
1 cup split Bengal gram, soaked overnight and drained
¾ cup grated jaggery pieces
1 teaspoon cardamom powder
1 cup whole wheat flour
½ cup all-purpose flour, plus more for rolling and dusting
4 tablespoons vegetable oil
4 tablespoons grated coconut
2 tablespoons yogurt

Cook the lentils in 3 cups water on medium heat in a large pan, until well cooked and soft.

Drain the excess water and transfer the lentils to a blender with the jaggery and cardamom powder. Blend to make a coarse paste. Reserve and set aside.

In a large mixing bowl combine the flours with 1 teaspoon of oil, the coconut, and the yogurt and mix well. Add about ¾ cup of water, a little at a time, to form a pliable dough. Cover with a damp kitchen towel and let it rest for at least 30 minutes at room temperature.

Divide the dough into 8 equal pieces. Working with one piece at a time, roll out the dough onto a lightly floured surface to a circle, 6 inches in diameter. Brush lightly with oil. Spoon the lentil mixture into the center of the round. Gather the edges and bring together in the center to form a pouch to enclose the filling. Press the ends together tightly to close the pouch. Once sealed, press down gently to flatten so that you have a flattened pouch. Roll this pouch into a 4-to-6-inch disc.

Heat a nonstick griddle over medium heat and lightly grease it. Place the rolled dough on the hot griddle and cook until each side is lightly browned, about 1 to 2 minutes on each side.

Remove the bread to a serving plate. Repeat the process with the remaining dough.

Garlic and Cinnamon Pathiri

These soft thin pancakes are made with rice flour and are a specialty of Kerala, especially the Mappilas, the Muslim community. There are many varieties of recipes for pathiri. They are usually eaten with curries and are prominent on the menus for Iftaar during Ramadan and other festivities.

If required, wet hands to knead dough, but adding extra water is not recommended as it changes the texture of the pathiri and makes a sticky dough, which is difficult to roll.

SERVES 6 TO 8
Salt to taste
2 tablespoons oil
3 cups roasted rice flour, plus more for rolling and dusting
4 cloves garlic, minced
½ teaspoon cinnamon powder

In a pan, boil 3 cups of water with the salt and 1 teaspoon of oil. Add the rice flour, minced garlic, and cinnamon and cook, stirring constantly, taking care the flour does not stick to the bottom or get burnt. Simmer for 45 to 50 seconds until all the water is absorbed and forms a soft dough.

Transfer to a work surface, and cautiously knead the dough thoroughly with your hands until smooth and less sticky. Pathiri will be softer if you knead it when the dough is still hot.

Roll out 6 to 8 portions of the dough into lime-sized balls and flatten slightly. With a rolling pin, roll each ball into thin discs about 6 inches in diameter.

Sprinkle a little rice flour on both sides of the discs and set aside on a plate.

Heat a nonstick griddle on medium heat and place a rolled out disc on it. Cook for 10 to 15 seconds and turn and cook for another 10 to 15 seconds. Press with the back of a spoon until the pathiri lightly puffs up. Make sure it does not brown.

Remove from the heat to a serving plate.

Clean the griddle to remove any brown dust before cooking the next pathiri. Repeat the process with the remaining dough.

Jala Bread with Carom Seeds

This recipe is inspired by the popular Malaysian street snack roti jala. Carom seeds add a sharp, pungent flavor to these crispy lacy breads. Adding buttermilk to the dough helps make them more light and fluffy. How fine and thin these crêpes turn out depends upon the smoothness of the batter, which should be as lump free as possible.

SERVES 6

1 cup all-purpose flour

1 teaspoon carom seeds, finely crushed

Salt to taste

1 teaspoon sugar

½ teaspoon turmeric

½ teaspoon chili powder

About 1 cup buttermilk

3 tablespoons vegetable oil

In a large mixing bowl, combine the flour, carom seeds, salt, sugar, turmeric, and chili powder and mix well. Add the buttermilk, a little at a time, stirring constantly until smooth, resembling the consistency of pancake batter.

Fill a squeeze bottle with the batter.

Heat oil in a frying pan over medium-high heat. Drizzle the batter onto the hot pan, making a lacy pattern. Cook until golden brown, about 2 to 3 minutes on each side.

Once the bread is cooked, slide it out of the pan onto a serving dish. Repeat the process with the remaining batter.

LENTILS

Green Lentils with Spinach and Chipotle

Green lentils combined with spinach are flavored with smoky chipotle, cardamom, and star anise. Glossy greenish brown lentils have a robust earthy flavor. They take longer to cook than most other lentil varieties, but they remain firm and do not get mushy when cooked.

SERVES 4 TO 6
1 cup green lentils, sorted and rinsed
Salt to taste
2 tablespoons vegetable oil
2 medium red onions, cut into 1-inch dices
2 cloves garlic, minced
1 whole star anise
3 whole cardamom pods
1 medium tomato, finely chopped
1 teaspoon ground chipotle chili or red pepper flakes
8 ounces fresh spinach leaves, coarsely chopped

Put the lentils and 1 teaspoon of salt in a saucepan with 3 cups of water. Bring to a boil on high heat, then reduce the heat to low and simmer, partially covered. Skim off any foam that forms on the surface. Cook until the lentils are tender, about 25 minutes. Drain and reserve.

Heat oil in a heavy-bottom pan over medium heat. Add the onions, garlic, star anise, and cardamom and sauté until the mixture is fragrant and the onions begin to caramelize around the edges, about 5 to 6 minutes.

Add the tomato and chipotle and cook until flavors are well combined.

Transfer the lentils to the pan with the broth and continue to cook until the flavors are well blended, 3 to 4 minutes. Stir in the spinach and cook for another minute.

Serve hot with rice or flat bread.

Herby Gingery Lentils

Salmon-hued pink lentils are cooked here with a mix of fresh herbs and coconut milk that adds to the complexity of flavors. The hull is removed from the lentils, which makes them cook fast and turn golden in color. Their texture is soft and silky, perfect for warm comforting soups. In this recipe, red or yellow lentils would work just as well.

SERVES 4 TO 6

1¼ cups pink lentils, sorted and rinsed
Salt to taste
1 teaspoon turmeric
2 tablespoons vegetable oil
1 red onion, finely chopped
One 2-inch fresh ginger, peeled and finely chopped
1 green chili, such as serrano, finely chopped
1 teaspoon cumin seeds
Pinch of asafoetida
6 to 8 curry leaves
½ cup coconut milk
3 tablespoons finely chopped fresh mint
3 tablespoons finely chopped fresh cilantro
3 tablespoons finely chopped fresh basil

Put the lentils and 1 teaspoon of salt and turmeric in a saucepan with 2 cups of water. Bring to a boil, then lower the heat and simmer, partially covered. Skim off any foam that forms on the surface. Cook until the lentils are tender and cooked through, about 15 to 20 minutes. Add more water if required. Remove from heat, transfer to a blender, and purée until smooth.

Heat the oil in a heavy-bottom pan over medium heat. Add the onions, ginger, chili, cumin, asafoetida, and curry leaves. Sauté until the mixture is fragrant and the onions are soft, about 3 to 4 minutes. Add the lentil purée with coconut milk and bring it to a boil on high heat.

Reduce the heat to low and simmer, stirring continuously until the lentils thicken. Garnish with the mint, cilantro, and basil and serve hot with flatbread or boiled rice.

Pomegranate-Flavored Chickpeas

Dried pomegranate seeds add a vibrant, tarty tanginess while the delicate and complex tea complements the nutty flavor of chickpeas. This curry dish tastes better the next day, as the chickpeas absorb the flavors of the spices and other ingredients.

SERVES 4 TO 6

2 tablespoons vegetable oil
1 large red onion, finely chopped
3 cloves garlic, minced
1½ tablespoons dried pomegranate seeds, coarsely ground
2 teaspoons coriander seeds, lightly crushed
1 dried red chili, crushed
1 large tomato, finely chopped
Salt to taste
2 cans (15.5 ounces) chickpeas, rinsed, drained, and patted dry
2 tea bags, preferably Darjeeling tea
½ cup fresh pomegranate seeds
3 to 4 chives, cut into 1-inch pieces

Heat the oil in a heavy-bottom skillet over medium heat. Add the onions, garlic, pomegranate seeds, coriander seeds, and red chili. Stir and cook until the onions begin to caramelize at the edges, about 3 to 4 minutes. Add the tomato and salt and continue to cook, stirring until the mixture becomes thick, about 3 minutes. Add the chickpeas and the tea bags with 1½ cups of water and bring to a boil. Reduce the heat to low, cover, and cook until the mixture begins to dry, about 6 to 8 minutes.

Remove the tea bags and, using the back of the spoon, mash the chickpeas slightly to thicken the mixture.

Serve hot, garnished with fresh pomegranate seeds and the chives.

Creamy Black-Eyed Peas with Roasted Garlic

Any variety of canned white beans can be used for this recipe. However, I like using black-eyed peas, for their delicate flavor and creamy texture. Seasoning with the rich flavor of garlic infuses the beans with a mellow, sweet, caramelized flavor and aroma.

SERVES 4 TO 6

2 tablespoons coconut or vegetable oil
1 teaspoon mustard seeds
1 teaspoon cumin seeds
5 cloves garlic, sliced
3 shallots, thinly sliced
2 cans (15. 5 ounces) black-eyed peas, rinsed, drained, and patted dry
Salt to taste
4 tablespoons chopped fresh cilantro
1 small red pepper, coarsely sliced
½ cup heavy cream
Freshly ground black pepper to taste
3 to 4 chives, finely chopped

Heat the oil in a large saucepan over medium heat. Add the mustard seeds and cumin and cook until they begin to crackle, about 1 minute. Be careful, as they could spatter hot oil.

Add the garlic, shallots, and 1 tablespoon of water, if required, to prevent the spices from burning. Cook until fragrant, about 2 minutes. Add the black-eyed peas, ½ cup of water, salt, cilantro, and red pepper and bring to a boil. Add the cream and black pepper and continue to cook for the desired consistency.

Serve hot, garnished with chives.

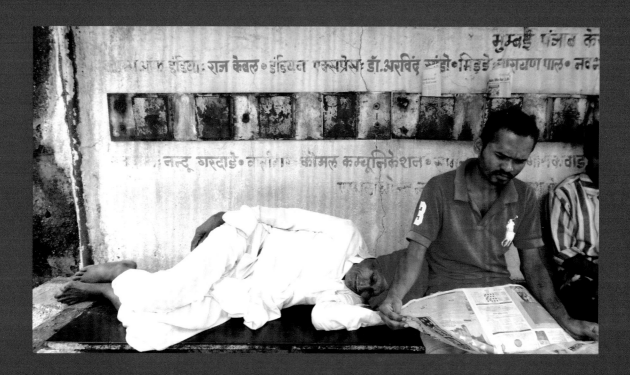

Red Beans with Round Gourd and Cinnamon

An interesting recipe for tender red kidney beans, featuring round gourd and the warm aroma of cinnamon. Fresh round gourd is one of my favorite vegetable because of its versatility. Sweet potato makes a good substitute for the sweet and creamy gourd. This dish makes for a delicious hearty meal, complete with a warm crusty bread.

SERVES 4 TO 6

2 tablespoons vegetable oil

6 medium tender round gourds, peeled, seeded, and cut into 1-inch cubes

1 teaspoon turmeric

One 2-inch cinnamon stick

Salt to taste

1 teaspoon sugar

1 can (15.5 ounces) red kidney beans, rinsed, drained, and patted dry

1 tablespoon chili flakes

Juice of 1 lemon

8 to 10 fresh cilantro leaves

Heat oil in a large saucepan over medium heat. Sauté round gourd, cinnamon, salt, and sugar for 2 minutes. Add the kidney beans and chili flakes and mix well. Add ½ cup of water and bring to a boil. Reduce heat and simmer, covered, until the mixture becomes dry, about 10 to 12 minutes. Add a little more water, if required.

Stir in the lemon juice and serve hot, garnished with the cilantro.

Spicy Orange-Mint Lentils

This healthy lentil recipe combines the refreshing citrus flavors of orange juice and fresh mint with the deep appetizing aromas of garlic, cumin, and fragrant curry leaves. Cream-colored white lentils are actually black lentils, split and skinned, and they have a wonderful, mild earthy flavor.

SERVES 4 TO 6

2 tablespoons canola oil
1 large red onion, finely chopped
1 teaspoon red chili powder
2 cloves garlic, minced
1 teaspoon cumin seeds
6 to 8 curry leaves
1 teaspoon turmeric
1 cup white lentils, rinsed and drained
Juice of 4 oranges, plus zest of 1
Salt to taste
2 tablespoons yogurt
¼ cup coarsely chopped fresh mint leaves

Heat the oil in a large saucepan over medium heat. Add the onions, chili, garlic, cumin, curry leaves, and turmeric and cook until fragrant, about 3 to 4 minutes.

Add the lentils, orange juice, and salt with ½ cup of water and bring to a boil. Reduce the heat to low and simmer, partially covered. Skim off any foam that forms on the surface. Cook until the lentils are tender, about 15 to 20 minutes. Add more water, if required. Remove from the heat and stir in the yogurt, orange zest, and mint.

Serve hot.

Tamarind Vegetable Lentils Medley

The rich, appetizing, and earthy flavors of split pigeon peas, or toor daal, make it an extremely popular lentil. A range of spices such as cumin, coriander seeds, asafoetida, mustard seed, and turmeric adds a delectable taste to this recipe, while tamarind adds just the right amount of tartness. Mixed vegetables make this a wholesome and healthy dish.

SERVE 4 TO 6
1 teaspoon cumin seeds
1 teaspoon coriander seeds
1 dried red chili
1 teaspoon black peppercorns
2 tablespoons vegetable or sunflower oil
1 teaspoon mustard seeds
Pinch of asafoetida
6 to 8 curry leaves
1 tomato, coarsely chopped
3 shallots, sliced
1 teaspoon turmeric
1 green chili, split
¾ cup split pigeon peas
1 cup mixed vegetables, such as peas, carrots, beans, or squash
2 tablespoons tamarind paste
10 to 12 fresh cilantro leaves

Dry roast the cumin, coriander, red chili, and black peppercorns in a skillet over low heat. Cook, stirring continuously until very fragrant, about 2 to 3 minutes. Remove from the heat and grind in a spice grinder.

Heat the oil in a large saucepan over medium heat. Add the mustard seeds, asafoetida, and curry leaves. Fry until fragrant, about 1 minute. Add the tomato, shallots, turmeric, green chili, spice mixture, and pigeon peas and 2 cups of water. Bring to a boil, reduce the heat to low, and simmer until the lentils are cooked but still firm, about 18 to 20 minutes.

Add the mixed vegetables, cover, and continue to cook until vegetables are cooked through, another 3 minutes. Add extra water if required. Stir in the tamarind paste and garnish with cilantro.

Serve hot with rice.

Lemony Black Chickpeas with Peppers and Plantain

The earthy-nutty flavor of black chickpeas gets a boost of aroma from warm cumin and soothing mustard seeds. Sweet and musky plantains pair well with the chickpeas, while mixed peppers add bright color and crunch to the dish.

SERVES 4 TO 6

1 cup black chickpeas, rinsed, soaked in 3 cups water overnight, and drained
Salt to taste
1 teaspoon turmeric
2 tablespoons coconut oil
1 teaspoon mustard seeds
1 red onion, thinly sliced
2 small plantains, peeled and cut into ⅓-inch-thick roundels
1 teaspoon cumin seeds
2 cloves garlic, minced
2 cups mixed peppers, cut into 1-inch cubes
2 scallions, coarsely chopped
1 teaspoon chili flakes
Juice of 1 lemon
1 green chili, finely chopped
6 to 8 chives, cut into 1-inch pieces

Put the black chickpeas, 1 teaspoon salt, and turmeric in a saucepan with 4 cups of water. Bring to a boil, then lower the heat and simmer, partially covered. Cook until the chickpeas are tender and cooked through but not mushy, about 45 to 50 minutes. Add more water if required. Drain and reserve.

In a medium saucepan, heat the coconut oil, the add the mustard seeds, onion, plantains, cumin, and garlic. Cook until the onions soften, about 3 to 4 minutes. Add the mixed peppers, scallions, chickpeas, salt, and chili flakes and stir well to evenly coat the peppers.

Stir in the lemon juice and green chilies and serve hot, garnished with chives.

CONDIMENTS

Green Mango Salsa

Green unripe mango pieces add a crunchy bite to this salsa without getting mushy. Cherries, combined with green mangoes, add bold colors plus a sweet-tart flavor. Sometimes I add seasonal fruits like strawberries, and some chilies will give it a spicy kick.

SERVES 1
Juice of 1 lime
1 large green mango, peeled, seeded and coarsely chopped
1 medium tomato, seeded and coarsely chopped
1 red onion, coarsely chopped
10 to 12 red cherries, seeded
Salt to taste
¼ cup coarsely chopped fresh mint

To make the salsa, combine all ingredients into a bowl and mix well.

Sprouted Lentil and Cumin Raita

Sprouted lentils are nutritious and an extremely versatile ingredient that can be added to salads, soups, and curries, or even used as a garnish. Sprouting lentils is very easy. The procedure of sprouting is almost the same for all grains and legumes, just the timing varies. Topped off with the smoky, woody flavors of toasted cumin, this raita is cooling, healthy, and delicious.

SERVES 2
1 cup mixed lentil sprouts
1 cup plain yogurt
Salt to taste
Freshly ground black pepper to taste
2 green chilies, chopped
¼ cup coarsely chopped mint leaves
1 teaspoon cumin seeds, lightly roasted

Mix all the ingredients together in a medium mixing bowl. Cover and chill in a refrigerator for 1 hour and serve.

Tamarind and Eggplant Raita

Raitas can be made using almost any kind of vegetable. The eggplant can be fried, as in this recipe, or grilled or roasted for a healthier option. Sweet and sour tamarind is added to the yogurt, seasoned with rich, warm, and smoky paprika.

SERVES 3
Vegetable oil for frying
1 medium eggplant, cut into 1-inch pieces
2 cups plain yogurt, whisked until smooth
1 teaspoon smoked paprika
1 tablespoon tamarind paste
Salt to taste
2 tablespoons finely chopped fresh cilantro
1 scallion, thinly sliced

Heat the oil to 350°F.

Gently fry the eggplant in batches until cooked through.

In a medium mixing bowl combine fried eggplant, yogurt, paprika, tamarind, salt, and cilantro and mix well.

Cover and chill.

Serve chilled, garnished with the scallion.

Crispy Okra Raita

Tempering with curry leaves and mustard seeds brings the classic South Indian flavor to this savory raita topped with crispy okra. Frying the okra makes it a nice, crunchy treat with the deliciously spiced yogurt.

SERVES 4
10 to 12 tender okra
2 tablespoons rice flour
Vegetable oil for frying, plus 2 tablespoons
1 teaspoon mustard seeds
1 teaspoon split gram
1 dried red chili, halved
¼ teaspoon asafoetida
4 to 6 curry leaves
2 cups plain yogurt, whisked until smooth
Salt to taste

Clean the okra with a damp kitchen towel and cut off both ends. Slice the okra lengthwise, toss with rice flour, and set aside.

Heat the vegetable oil to 350°F. Fry the cut okra until crispy, remove with a slotted spoon, and drain onto a paper towel.

Heat the oil in a small pan over medium heat and fry the mustard seeds, split gram, chili, asafoetida, and curry leaves until the mustard seeds start crackling and the mixture is very fragrant. Remove from the heat and let cool. Add the spice mixture to the yogurt with salt and mix well.

Divide the yogurt among 6 dip bowls, garnish with the fried okra, and serve immediately.

Crispy Spinach Raita with Pomegranate

In this refreshing raita, fresh ruby red pomegranate seeds add a tangy bite and texture along with the goodness of spinach greens. I generally add spinach just before serving, or sometimes even serve it on the side, so that it doesn't lose its crunchiness.

SERVES 4
Vegetable oil for deep frying
½ pound fresh baby spinach, washed and patted dry
2 cups sour cream
1 small onion, thinly sliced
1 teaspoon cumin seeds, roasted and ground
¼ teaspoon red chili powder
Freshly ground black pepper to taste
Salt to taste
½ cup fresh pomegranate seeds

Heat the vegetable oil to 350°F.

Fry the spinach until crispy, remove with a slotted spoon, and drain onto a paper towel.

Combine the sour cream with onion, cumin, chili powder, pepper, and salt and whisk well.

To serve, spoon dollops of spiced sour cream into a bowl, garnish with the pomegranate and fried spinach, and serve immediately.

Zucchini and Lime Raita

The beautiful golden zucchini is slightly sweeter and has a firmer texture than the subtle flavors of the slightly softer green zucchini. The lime juice marinade with chilies and garlic infuses a tangy zest of flavor. However, do not the marinate zucchini for too long as it will lose its firmness because of the acidity of the lime juice. I like to layer the zucchini on top of the yogurt, rather than mix it in, which gives it a great visual appeal.

SERVES 4
1 large green zucchini, thinly sliced
1 large yellow zucchini, thinly sliced
2 tablespoons olive oil
Juice of 2 limes
4 large cloves garlic
1 teaspoon red chili flakes
½ teaspoon crushed peppercorns
Sea salt to taste
2 cups Greek yogurt
2 scallions, thinly sliced

Combine sliced zucchini with olive oil, lime juice, garlic, chili flakes, pepper, and salt. Toss well and keep aside to marinate for 5 minutes.

Heat a grill pan, grease with the prepared marinade, and arrange the marinated zucchini in a single layer. Grill the zucchini on both sides until grill marks appear clearly.

In a mixing bowl, combine yogurt with salt and pepper. Spoon the yogurt in an even layer on a platter. Layer the grilled zucchini, alternating green and yellow over the yogurt, and drizzle the remaining marinade over it.

Serve immediately, garnished with the scallions.

Plantain Jaggery Chutney

In South Indian cuisine plantains are cooked in jaggery, which adds more color and sweetness to them. This sweetness balances off two layers of spiciness added by peppercorns and red chilies in this recipe. This chutney could also be puréed and added as a marinade to create an intense flavor for grilled vegetables. I sometimes add a spoonful of this chutney while simmering vegetables to create delicious curries.

MAKES ABOUT 3 CUPS
½ **cup grated jaggery**
⅔ **cup white wine vinegar**
1 teaspoon cardamom seeds
½-**inch cinnamon stick**
5 cloves
8 black peppercorns
10 cloves garlic
One 2-inch fresh ginger, peeled and coarsely chopped
10 to 15 dried red chilies
1 tablespoon vegetable oil
1 teaspoon ground turmeric
4 ripe plantains, peeled and sliced lengthwise
2 tablespoons black mustard seeds, ground to a powder
Salt to taste

Soak the jaggery in the wine vinegar. Combine the cardamom seeds, cinnamon, cloves, peppercorns, garlic, ginger, and chilies in a spice grinder and grind to a paste with a little water.

Heat the oil, add ground paste and turmeric, and fry for 1 minute. Add the plantains and cook until soft. Add the jaggery, wine vinegar mixture, mustard, and salt and stir well, then simmer over low heat until the mixture comes together. Leave to cool. Store in airtight jars and refrigerate.

Citrusy Orange and Raisin Chutney

An easy recipe with an undertone of spices added to the citrusy flavors of orange and balanced by the sweet fruitiness of the dates. Seltzer water can be added to a spoonful of this chutney to make a tasty drink. The sparkle of the seltzer water creates a fizziness that brings out the wonderful flavors of the oranges and spicy cayenne. You can also store this chutney in sterilized airtight jars and refrigerate for up to a month.

MAKES ABOUT 2 CUPS
6 to 8 oranges, such as navel, cut into segments
1 red onion, chopped
⅔ cup golden raisins
¾ cup granulated sugar, or to taste
1 teaspoon salt
Pinch of cayenne pepper
½ cup malt vinegar

Combine the oranges in a large pan with all the remaining ingredients on medium-high heat. Reduce the heat to low and stir until the sugar has dissolved. Simmer gently, stirring occasionally for about 15 to 20 minutes until the mixture comes together.

Serve fresh.

Star Fruit and Ginger Pickle

The firm texture and tangy flavor of the star-shaped, tropical star fruit make it perfect for pickles. Usually vegetables are sun dried while making pickles; however, here they are cooked on the stove top to speed up the preparation. It is additionally flavored with spicy ginger and aromatic asafoetida and the earthy flavors of sesame oil.

MAKES ABOUT 1 CUP
1 teaspoon fenugreek seeds
2 tablespoons sesame seed oil
½ teaspoon asafoetida
2 teaspoons mustard seeds
½ teaspoon ground turmeric
4 teaspoons chili powder
One 5-inch fresh ginger, peeled and sliced
4 to 6 star fruits, sliced
Salt to taste
3 tablespoons sugar

Dry roast the fenugreek seeds on medium-low heat in a small pan until darker in color. Cool and grind to a powder.

Heat oil in a medium pan over medium heat and add the asafoetida and mustard seeds. When the mustard crackles, add the remaining ingredients and cook for a few minutes, stirring until flavors are well blended.

Serve hot or at room temperature.

Mango and Cranberry Chutney

Chutneys are a great accompaniment to savory snacks and vegetables. Summer is a great time for mango lovers like me, as there are so many varieties available. I served this chutney in the summer of 2007 at my restaurant in New York in a tasting menu called "Tango with Mango" for a special celebration of the fruit.

MAKES 2 CUPS
4 green mangoes
1 cup fresh or frozen cranberries (thawed if frozen)
One 2-inch fresh ginger, peeled and grated
4 tablespoons maple syrup
½ cup vinegar
2 tablespoons chili powder
2 teaspoons salt

Peel and slice the mangoes.

Combine all the ingredients in a heavy-bottom pan over medium heat. Simmer, stirring occasionally until all the flavors blend and the mangoes are tender but still firm, about 15 minutes.

Leave to cool. Transfer to sterilized airtight jars. This chutney can be stored in the refrigerator for up to a month.

PRESERVED FOR FLAVORS

In many parts of India, condiments or pickles are the identity of the kitchen. These condiments not only capture and preserve the flavor of the fruit and seasonings, but they are an essential part of the meals.

Sweet, salty, spicy, sour, and pungent, the fruits and vegetables are picked at the height of the season when the flavors are in their prime and are then, interestingly, sealed away to be enjoyed for the rest of the year.

The flavor of the jam as it is spread on nice crusty toast or a stale piece of flatbread brightens up any morning for me.

Right after dust storms, we would run to collect raw mangoes that had fallen off the tree. Some would go straight to our stomach and some to the kitchen. The ones that made it to the kitchen would be turned into fresh cooling mango drinks and sometimes mango pickles with mustard oil, fennel, and nigella seeds after they were fermented in the sun.

Peach and Bay Leaves Chutney

Aromatic bay leaves bring out the warm taste in this sweet and spicy fruit chutney made with ripe juicy peaches and tart red currants. The pungent and lemony undertones of ginger add another flavor to this great side dish.

MAKES ABOUT 2 CUPS
6 peaches, stoned and sliced
⅔ cup red currants
2 medium red onion, finely chopped
One 1-inch fresh ginger, peeled and finely chopped
Salt to taste
3 tablespoons sugar, or to taste
3 large bay leaves
Finely grated rind and juice of 1 lemon

Combine all ingredients in a medium saucepan and cook over medium heat until the peaches are mushy and the flavors are well blended. Leave to cool. Store in a sterilized glass jar for up to a month in the refrigerator.

Guava and Fenugreek Relish

This condiment captures the exotic sweetness and musky aromas of soft ripe guavas. Lime juice and cilantro also add to the main flavors of the relish, making it a fresh citrusy accompaniment to the main dish it is served with.

MAKES ABOUT 1½ CUPS
4 ripe guavas, seeded and cut into wedges
2 tablespoons vegetable oil
1 teaspoon black salt
1 teaspoon dried fenugreek leaves
One 2-inch piece fresh turmeric, peeled and sliced
4 green chilies, halved
4 tablespoons lemon juice

Toss the guavas with the oil and salt. Heat a grill pan over medium-high heat and grill the guavas until marks appear. Toss the grilled guavas with the remaining ingredients and serve.

Custard Apple and Coconut Chutney

The sweet and creamy floral flavors of custard apples are a perfect complement to the rich tropical flavors of coconut. White wine vinegar is used to add a delicate yet mellow sourness and acid in this preserve. Sometimes I substitute bananas for custard apples, which also work very well.

MAKES ABOUT 1½ CUPS
2 ripe custard apples, pulp removed
1 cup freshly grated coconut
4 tablespoons chopped fresh mint
2 tablespoons white wine vinegar
Coarse salt to taste
Freshly ground black pepper to taste
10 to 12 fresh mint leaves

Combine all the ingredients and toss well.

Serve chilled.

Green Tomato and Pineapple Relish

A Thai-inspired recipe that combines the sour unripe, green tomatoes and the sweet, juicy pineapple with the beautiful color, aroma, and light peppery taste of pink peppercorns. I like to add extra basil leaves for their light, refreshing flavor.

MAKES 2 CUPS
1 cup diced pineapple
2 green tomatoes, diced
½ fresh red chili, seeded and finely chopped
2 tablespoons lime juice
1 teaspoon dried pink peppercorns
Salt to taste
¼ cup fresh basil leaves

Toss all the ingredients together and set aside for an hour to allow the flavors to merge. Fill a sterilized glass jar and refrigerate.

Serve chilled.

Green Apple and Garlic Pickle

The sourness of green apple combines wonderfully with the flavor of garlic. You can leave the garlic cloves whole as well and add ginger. Sugarcane juice brings a refreshing mild sweetness to the pickle, but you can also substitute it with any other juice you prefer.

MAKES ABOUT 2 CUPS
4 green apples, cored and diced
2 fresh red chilies, sliced
4 to 6 garlic cloves, chopped
1 teaspoon ground turmeric
½ teaspoon allspice berries
1 cup freshly squeezed sugarcane juice
1 tablespoon sugar
Salt to taste

Combine the the ingredients in a saucepan and cook over medium-low heat until the apples soften and the flavors merge. Leave to cool. Fill sterilized glass jars and store in a refrigerator.

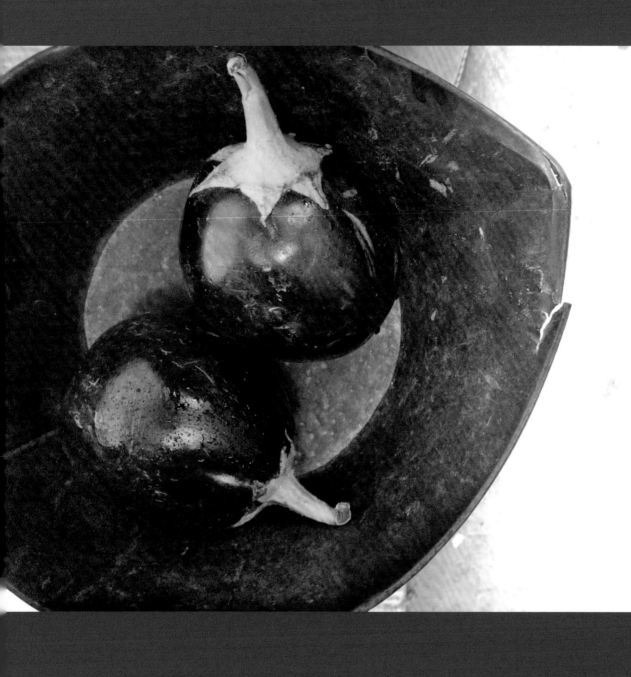

DESSERTS

Mixed Berry Salad with Maple Butter

Sweet-tart juicy berries add an abundance of bright delicious flavors to this recipe. Served with creamy, warm maple butter laced with cinnamon, this makes a memorable dessert.

SERVES 4
1 tablespoon balsamic vinegar
2 teaspoons dark brown sugar
1½ cups strawberries, hulled and halved or quartered
¾ cup raspberries
½ cup blackberries
2 tablespoons small mint leaves, plus sprigs for garnish
½ cup softened butter
¼ cup maple syrup
½ teaspoon ground cinnamon
Juice of 1 lemon

In a medium bowl, whisk together vinegar and sugar. Add strawberries, raspberries, blackberries, and mint leaves and toss well.

In a medium mixing bowl combine butter, maple syrup, cinnamon, and lemon juice. Using an electric mixer combine until smooth and creamy.

Top the berries with the maple butter and serve chilled.

Lemon Cream with Blackberries

The refreshing citrus scent and flavors of lemongrass are a great accompaniment to fresh blackberries. Silken tofu is an important ingredient in dairy-free recipes. It has a wonderful soft and creamy texture which is the perfect level of consistency for this dessert.

SERVES 4
1 stalk lemongrass, coarsely chopped
¼ cup sugar
½ cup freshly squeezed orange juice
1 lemon, zested and juiced
½ cup honey
1 cup drained silken tofu
1 cup blackberries
8 to 10 fresh mint leaves

In a small medium pan, combine the lemongrass, sugar, and orange juice and bring to a boil on medium-high heat. Remove from heat and let it stand at room temperature for at least 30 minutes. Strain and reserve.

In a blender purée the orange mixture, lemon juice, honey, and tofu and process until smooth and creamy.

Cover and refrigerate until chilled, about an hour.

To serve, layer the serving dish with orange-tofu mixture and garnish with the blackberries, mint leaves, and lemon zest.

Roasted Peaches with Brown Sugar

Roasting is a great cooking technique and makes fruits tender while intensifying the sweetness. In addition, the pieces here are glazed with a spicy-sweet flavor from the cayenne and sugar. The layer of creamy annatto-infused yogurt is a great complement to the peaches.

SERVES 4

1 teaspoon annatto
¼ cup hot milk
1 cup Greek yogurt
3 tablespoons honey
4 tablespoons dark brown sugar
One 2-inch fresh ginger, peeled and minced
1 teaspoon cayenne pepper
Juice of 1 lemon
6 ripe peaches, pitted and quartered
3 to 4 tips of basil sprigs

Combine the annatto with milk and mix well. Strain and reserve the milk. Refrigerate until chilled, about an hour.

In a medium mixing bowl, combine the Greek yogurt, honey, and annatto mixture until smooth and creamy. Cover and refrigerate.

Preheat oven to 350°F.

In a medium mixing bowl stir together sugar, ginger, ½ teaspoon of cayenne pepper, and lemon juice.

Toss in the peaches and mix to evenly coat them with the spice mixture.

Arrange the peaches on a baking sheet.

Bake the peaches until bubbling and the edges begin to darken, about 15 minutes.

Remove from the oven and serve warm over the Greek yogurt mixture, garnished with the basil leaves and reserved cayenne pepper.

Cardamom-Scented Sweet Rice Balls

These subtly spiced rice balls are flavored with warm and aromatic cardamom, vanilla, and cinnamon. Cardamom is considered the queen of spices, and this aromatic spice adds a rich intoxicating lemony flavor. I like to grind it fresh right before adding it to the recipe since storing it for too long makes it lose its flavor and aroma.

SERVES 4 TO 6

1 cup cooked basmati rice
4 tablespoons brown sugar
2 teaspoons cardamom seeds, coarsely ground
A pinch of ground cinnamon
2 teaspoons vanilla extract
About ½ cup rice flour
Vegetable oil for frying
2 teaspoons baking powder
About ¼ cup warm milk
1 cup dried unsweetened coconut flakes
Cocoa powder for dusting

Place the cooked rice, sugar, cardamom, cinnamon, and vanilla extract in a large bowl and whisk to combine. Sift in the flour and baking powder. Gradually add the milk and mix well to form a soft dough.

Heat the oil to 325°F.

Make small balls of the mixture and roll them in coconut flakes. Fry the balls in batches until evenly golden in color and cooked through.

Carefully remove with a slotted spoon and drain onto a paper towel to remove excess oil.

Serve hot with chocolate or vanilla ice cream, dusted with the cocoa powder.

Ginger Cake with Pistachios

Ginger cake is a classic British teatime pastry. This light and crusty cake is spiced with licorice flavors of star anise and crunchy pistachios. It makes for a most elegant meal when served with a dollop of fresh crème fraîche and a cup of steaming hot orange pekoe tea.

SERVES 4 TO 6
2 cups all-purpose flour
One 2-inch fresh ginger, peeled and minced
½ cup unsalted butter, softened, plus more for greasing
1 cup pistachios, shelled
1¼ cups heavy cream
1 teaspoon baking soda
1 teaspoon white vinegar

Sift the flour and the spices. Add the butter and combine until the mixture resembles fine bread crumbs. Stir in the pistachios and cream and combine until the mixture is soft.

In a small mixing bowl, combine the baking soda and vinegar and whisk it until the mixture froths. Add it to the cake mixture.

Preheat oven to 350°F.

Grease a shallow baking pan with parchment paper and transfer the cake mixture to the pan.

Bake in the oven for 50 to 60 minutes until the cake is cooked through and when a skewer inserted in the center comes out clean.

Leave in the pan for 15 minutes, then place on a wire rack to cool. Serve warm or at room temperature.

318

THE SWEET LIFE

"Let's distribute ladoos"—this is one of the first things we say when we hear good news in India. Ladoos are round sweet balls.

I have tasted ladoos from every part of the country and I love them all! Though the main ingredient would vary—from coconut to rice; from whole wheat flour to chickpea flour; with or without dried fruits—no matter what the occasion, it is always celebrated with ladoos.

In India, a little baby with healthy round cheeks is also called "ladoo."

I used to love visiting the temple especially for the sweet prashad or the food offered to the gods. Each time we were leaving the house to start a journey or to take an exam, we were given a pinch of sugar for good luck and safe returns.

Whether I was working with halwais or the sweet vendors on the streets in India or the top pastry chefs in France, one thing is for sure: we were all patrons of the delicious sweet side of life.

Rose-Cinnamon Poached Apricots

I always found the undertones of citrusy lemon zest combined with the floral aroma of rose very addictive. The festive cinnamon adds a whole new dimension of taste as it cooks with the fruit. Velvety and tender apricots are a treat for any feast, served hot or chilled.

SERVES 4 TO 6
½ **cup honey**
1 lemon, peeled and juiced, zest reserved
One 2-inch cinnamon stick
10 to 12 fresh edible rose petals or ¼ **teaspoon rose water**
6 firm apricots, peeled, pitted, and halved
½ **cup fresh coconut, lightly toasted**

In a medium saucepan, bring 1 cup of water, honey, lemon peels, cinnamon, and rose petals to a boil on high heat. Reduce the heat to low and add apricots and lemon juice. Cook for another minute then remove from heat and cool at room temperature.

Cover and refrigerate until cool.

Serve chilled with vanilla or coconut ice cream, garnished with toasted coconut.

Apple Saffron Cake

A super moist and gooey cake made with sweet crisp apples. The warm earthiness of saffron, a versatile spice, works well with both savory dishes and desserts. Saffron brings out the color and flavor highlights in the buttery glaze.

SERVES 4 TO 6
1 teaspoon saffron threads
1 cup sugar
¼ cup unsalted butter, softened
3 large Gala apples, peeled, cored, and cut into ¼-inch-thick slices
¼ cup heavy cream
1½ cups all-purpose flour
3 tablespoons unsweetened cocoa powder
1 teaspoon baking soda
1 cup sugar
Zest of 1 orange
5 tablespoons olive oil, plus more for greasing
1 cup plain yogurt, whisked until smooth
1 tablespoon apple cider vinegar

In a coffee or spice grinder pulse the saffron and ¼ cup of sugar until well combined. Using an electric mixer, combine the butter and saffron-sugar mixture until it becomes frothy and smooth.

Heat the mixture in a medium heavy-bottom pan on medium heat. Cook, stirring until the sugar begins to caramelize, about 3 to 4 minutes. Add the apples and let it cook on low heat until soft, about 2 minutes. Stir in the cream and gently mix. Remove from heat.

Preheat the oven to 350°F.

Mix together the flour, cocoa powder, baking soda, sugar, and orange zest. Add the oil, yogurt, and vinegar and mix well using a hand blender, making sure there are no lumps in the batter.

Pour the batter in a 9-inch round or square greased baking pan.

Bake for 30 to 40 minutes or until a wooden pick inserted in the center comes out clean. Cool in the pan on a wire rack for 5 minutes. Carefully run a knife around the edge of the cake to loosen. Invert cake onto a serving plate. Arrange the apples on the cake, spooning all the juices in the pan over the cake.

Serve hot or at room temperature.

Persimmon-Vanilla Cobbler

Cobbler is one of my favorite desserts, and is easy to make with many fruit combinations. In this recipe, the tangy sweet delicate flavor of persimmons is enhanced by rich, smooth vanilla and topped with buttery crispy pastry—a comforting end to a perfect meal.

SERVES 4 TO 6

8 persimmons, trimmed and cut into wedges
1 teaspoon vanilla extract
½ cup brown sugar
1¼ cups plus 2 tablespoons all-purpose flour
6 tablespoons cold unsalted butter, cut into pieces
1 teaspoon baking powder
1 tablespoon cornstarch
¼ cup thinly slivered skinless almonds
Pinch of salt

Heat oven to 350°F.

In a bowl, toss the persimmons with the vanilla extract, ¼ cup of sugar, and 2 tablespoons of flour. Transfer to a medium baking dish.

Combine the remaining flour and ¼ cup sugar with the butter, baking powder, cornstarch, almonds, and salt, using your fingers to form coarse crumbs.

Evenly cover the persimmon layers with the mixture without pressing it.

Place the baking dish on a rimmed baking sheet and bake until golden brown and bubbly, 50 to 60 minutes.

Serve hot with vanilla ice cream.

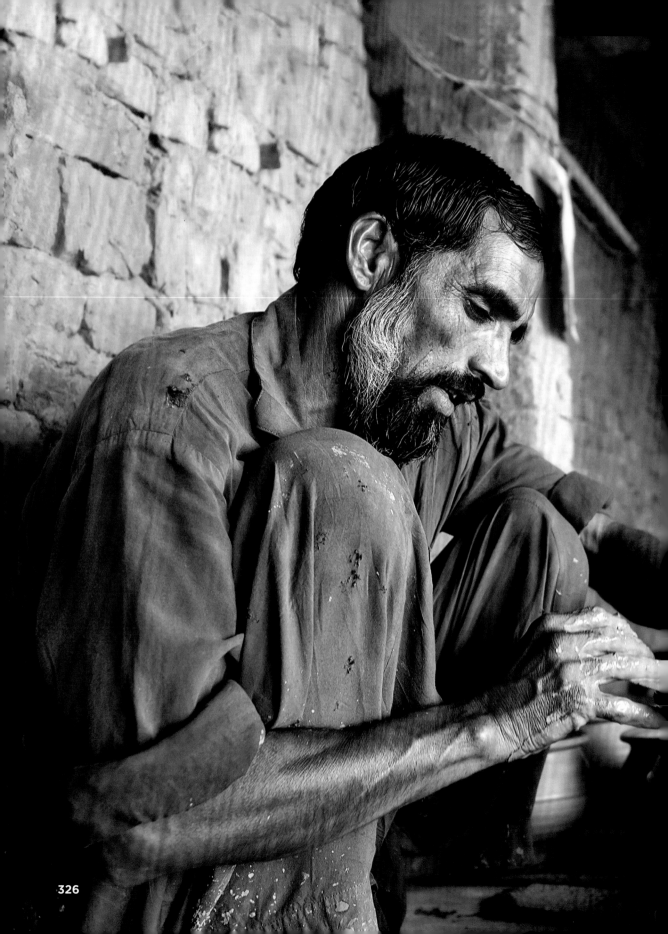

IT ALL BEGINS HERE AND ENDS WITH HER

We were all taught Kabir's writings in school. Kabir was a saint and mystic poet, and his writings have greatly influenced the culture in India. Though we had to remember all the dohas (couplets) in Hindi, I could not remember any except for this one (below), which later became my favorite. I would use it during my conversations and debates, just to look intelligent.

Maati kahe kumhaar se, tu kya ronde mohe
Ik din aisa aayega, main raundungo tohe
The earth says to the potter, "Why are you trampling me?"
One day, it will so happen that I will trample you.

The couplet signifies that we must be humble and not arrogant and that what we do to others will come back to us.

At another level, it is also true that we rise from the soil and we merge into it. Everything that brings things to life is the soil and then everything disappears into the soil.

Strawberry Lime Tangy Yogurt

A light and feathery dessert with the lush flavor of sweet-and-sour strawberries and tangy lime, this tastes great by itself or as a topping on pies or puddings. You can make this dessert with any fruit of your choice. Sometimes I like to top it with toasted nuts or crunchy granola.

SERVES 4

8 ounces fresh strawberries, rinsed, hulled, and halved
Juice of 2 limes
½ cup superfine sugar
1 cup hung or Greek yogurt
½ teaspoon vanilla extract
¼ cup heavy cream, whipped
Rosemary sprigs
1 lemon, cut into thin wedges

Place the strawberries in a bowl and sprinkle with the juice of 1 lime and 1 tablespoon of superfine sugar. Let rest at room temperature for 10 minutes.

In a medium mixing bowl, combine the remaining sugar, Greek yogurt, vanilla extract, and whipped cream.

Cover and chill for at least 3 hours and serve with the strawberry mixture, rosemary sprigs, and lemon wedges.

Caramelized Banana Rice Pudding

This creamy rice pudding offers up a mélange of flavors—sweet and earthy jaggery, the rich tropical flavor of coconut, and warm cinnamon. Caramelizing the bananas with brown sugar draws out its nutty and deep flavors, while deglazing the pan with orange juice adds another layer of citrusy undertones.

SERVES 6
2 cups cooked short grain rice, rinsed and drained
½ cup grated jaggery
2 cups unsweetened coconut milk
½ teaspoon vanilla extract
¼ cup raisins
¼ cup almonds, coarsely chopped
2 medium firm bananas, peeled and coarsely chopped
1 tablespoon butter
3 tablespoons light brown sugar
1 orange, zested and juiced
⅛ teaspoon ground cinnamon
10 to 12 fresh mint leaves

Preheat the oven to 350°F.

In a medium bowl, combine rice, jaggery, coconut milk, vanilla, raisins, and almonds and stir well. Transfer the mixture to a baking dish or an ovenproof pan. Bake for about 30 to 40 minutes until the pudding is thick. Cool at room temperature, cover, and refrigerate overnight.

Melt butter in a nonstick skillet over medium-high heat. Add brown sugar and cook until it begins to caramelize, about 3 minutes. Add the bananas and cook, stirring for a minute. Add the orange juice and cinnamon and cook until hot.

Serve immediately over rice pudding, garnished with the orange zest and mint leaves.

जैसा भोजन कीजयि, वैसा ही मन होय।
जैसा पानी पीजयि, तैसी वाणी होय।।

—संत कबीर

YOUR SOUL IS AFFECTED BY THE FOOD YOU EAT.

YOUR VOICE AND BEHAVIOR IS IMPACTED BY THE

WATER YOU DRINK.

—SANT KABIR

DRINKS

Gingery Lemonade

A simple and delightful drink; the ginger provides a pungency, which is balanced by the sourness of the lemon. A nice twist to a classic, this drink can be made well in advance and also stored.

MAKES 4 TO 6 CUPS
4 tablespoons sugar
Juice of 4 lemons, or to taste
2 tablespoons fresh ginger juice
Pinch of salt
15 to 20 tips of mint sprigs

Combine the sugar, lemon juice, ginger juice, salt, and 3 cups of cold water in a blender.

Add 2 cups of ice and blend until the mixture is smooth and slushy. Add more water or ice until the texture is to your liking.

Garnish with mint and serve.

Green Mango and Mint Cooler

As the days become longer and we enter the summer, for me the greatest joy is the season of green mangoes. Green mangoes are used in a variety of recipes, such as curries, pickles, and also cooling drinks such as this one.

MAKES ABOUT 4 CUPS
1 medium green mango
1 teaspoon cumin seeds, roasted
1 teaspoon black salt
3 tablespoons honey, or to taste
1 teaspoon chaat masala
3 tablespoons sugar, or to taste
1 tablespoon finely chopped mint leaves
2 lime wedges

Bring 3 cups of water to a boil on high heat. Add the mango, reduce the heat to low, and simmer until the mango is tender, about 10 to 15 minutes.

Remove the mango from the water and set aside to cool. Then peel and remove all the flesh, using a sharp knife and a spoon. Reserve the pulp.

Place the mango pulp, cumin seeds, black salt, honey, and chaat masala powder into a blender and process until smooth.

Add 3 cups of water to the mango mixture, cover, and refrigerate until chilled.

Spread the sugar and mint leaves on a plate. Moisten the rim of a glass with a lime wedge. Turn the glass upside down and dip it into the mixture of sugar and mint to evenly cover the rim. Gently pour the mango drink into the glass over ice and serve.

Spicy Mandarin Cilantro

As you travel during summer in North India, one comes across street carts carrying earthen pots covered with a red cloth, serving cool drinks to weary travelers. It rejuvenates and hydrates at the same time. Tabasco is used in a number of cocktails, and when added in this recipe, it offers a nice hint of spiciness. When adding a hot spice to your recipes, be sure to adjust the level of heat to suit your palate.

MAKES 4 CUPS
4 cups freshly squeezed mandarin juice
2 teaspoons chili powder
1 teaspoon chili sauce, such as tabasco
Pinch of salt
Fresh cilantro leaves for garnish

Combine the juice, chili powder, chili sauce, and salt in a jug and refrigerate for at least 1 hour. The longer it is chilled, the more the flavors develop.

Pour into glasses with ice and garnish with cilantro leaves.

Plum Juice with Honey and Chaat Masala

I love the citrusy-salty aroma of chaat masala in drinks and appetizers. I prefer using fresh plums for this recipe, because they not only add a wonderful layer to the flavor, but they are also very high in antioxidants. Add a little extra honey if you like your drink on the sweeter side.

MAKES 4 CUPS

3 cups freshly squeezed plum juice, plus wedges for garnish

4 tablespoons lime juice

1 teaspoon honey

1 teaspoon chaat masala

Mix together the plum juice, lime juice, honey, and chaat masala in a jug.

Chill for 1 hour to enhance the flavors.

Serve chilled garnished with plum wedges.

Kiwi-Mint Smoothie

Green is the color of a fresh and invigorating drink. I like to freeze this mixture into ice cubes, which I then crush and serve in small glasses. Coral-colored Indian black salt is often used in cool summer drinks adding a burst of smoky tanginess. The black kiwi seeds add a wonderful bite and distinct presentation to this drink.

MAKES 4 CUPS
8 to 10 ripe kiwis, plus more for garnish
½ cup freshly squeezed lemon juice
1 teaspoon cumin seeds, roasted and coarsely ground
2 pinches of black salt
10 mint leaves
2 tablespoons honey, or to taste

Carefully peel the kiwis with a paring knife and coarsely chop them.

Transfer the kiwis to a blender and add the lemon juice, cumin seeds, black salt, mint, and honey and blend until smooth. Add water as required to smoothe the mixture.

Serve chilled garnished with kiwi slices.

Soy Milk Ginger Smoothie

I love the peppery combination of radish and smooth, creamy, earthy soy milk. For a milder taste and bite, you can also use French breakfast radish. I have also tried making this drink with buttermilk instead of soy milk and it works very well.

MAKES 4 CUPS
3 cups soy milk
2 tablespoons fresh ginger juice
2 tablespoons honey, or to taste
Pinch of nutmeg
10 to 12 red radishes, trimmed and coarsely chopped
Small bunch of micro radish

Combine the soy milk, ginger juice, honey, nutmeg, and radishes in a blender and process until smooth.

Serve chilled or over ice, garnished with micro radish.

Cinnamon Fennel Chai

Rejuvenate yourself with this flavor of chai at any time of the day. I generally make this tea in large quantities and add milk when required. You can also serve this wonderful chai chilled over ice. Feel free to substitute your choice of spices to make your own version.

MAKES 4 CUPS
2 tablespoons black tea
3 cloves
2 whole star anise
One 2-inch cinnamon stick
1 teaspoon fennel seeds
¼ cup whole milk, or to taste
2 tablespoons sugar, or to taste

Bring 4 cups of water to a boil in a medium pan on high heat. Add the tea and cook for a minute. Reduce the heat to low and add the cloves, star anise, cinnamon, and fennel and simmer until fragrant, about 2 to 3 minutes. Add the milk and continue to cook for your desired taste.

Strain and serve hot with the sugar on the side.

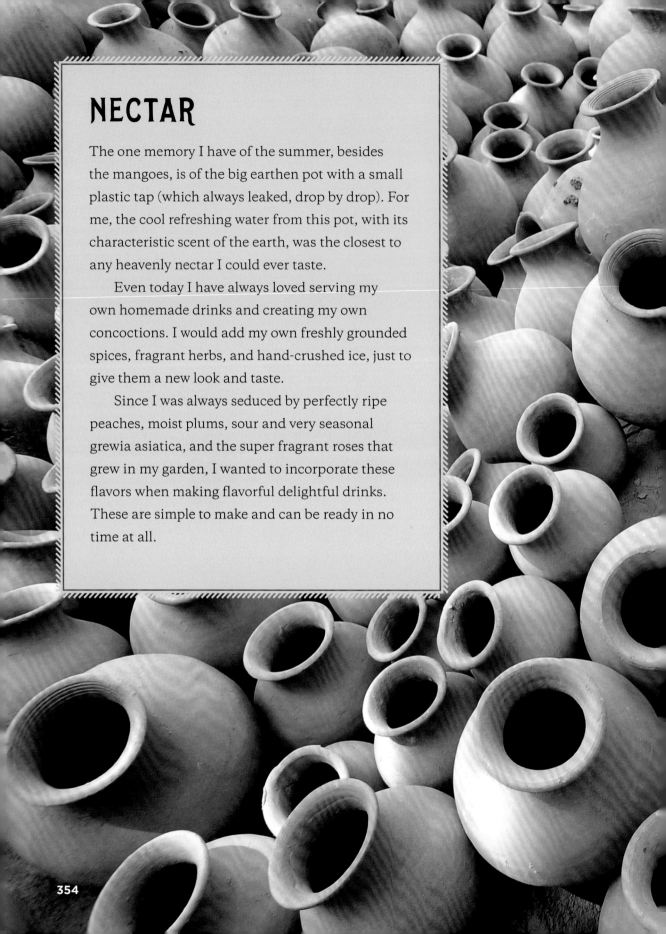

NECTAR

The one memory I have of the summer, besides the mangoes, is of the big earthen pot with a small plastic tap (which always leaked, drop by drop). For me, the cool refreshing water from this pot, with its characteristic scent of the earth, was the closest to any heavenly nectar I could ever taste.

Even today I have always loved serving my own homemade drinks and creating my own concoctions. I would add my own freshly grounded spices, fragrant herbs, and hand-crushed ice, just to give them a new look and taste.

Since I was always seduced by perfectly ripe peaches, moist plums, sour and very seasonal grewia asiatica, and the super fragrant roses that grew in my garden, I wanted to incorporate these flavors when making flavorful delightful drinks. These are simple to make and can be ready in no time at all.

Avocado and Mango with Black Pepper

Avocados add a rich, buttery creaminess to this drink. The sweet, ripe mangoes and the slight spiciness of black pepper make this drink delicious. It's also highly nutritious and a new favorite in nonalcoholic drinks. If you prefer a thinner consistency, you can add a little milk.

MAKES 4 CUPS
3 large soft, ripe avocados
2 ripe mangoes, peeled and flesh removed, plus wedges for garnish
1½ cups plain yogurt
½ teaspoon vanilla extract
2 tablespoons sugar
Pinch of salt
Pinch of black cracked pepper

Combine the avocados, mango, yogurt, vanilla, sugar, and salt in a blender with 1 cup of water and blend until smooth. Cover and chill in the refrigerator.

Transfer to a serving glass, sprinkle with the black pepper, and garnish with mango wedges.

Berry Beet Medley

When I am in the mood for a quick, healthy on-the-go meal, I generally make this shake. It is a toast to a nutritious vegetarian diet. Feel free to add fruits of your choice to give it a natural sweetness. I generally keep the vegetables and fruits covered in the refrigerator, ready to be juiced fresh for this energy booster.

MAKES 4 TO 6 CUPS
6 to 8 medium beets, trimmed and peeled
2 to 3 carrots, peeled
10 to 12 grapes
1 cup mixed berries
2 teaspoons honey, or to taste

Juice all the vegetables and fruits through a juicer.

Mix in the honey and serve fresh.

Passion Fruit and Star Anise Batida

This drink is inspired by the popular Brazilian cocktail made with liquor from fermented sugarcane juice. In Portuguese, "batida" means shaken or blended. The intense aromatic flavor of the passion fruit added to the condensed milk adds a special tang. It combines well with the licorice flavor of star anise. This is my version of that classic drink.

MAKES 4 TO 6 CUPS
6 to 8 passion fruits, halved
¼ cup condensed milk
2 cups fresh sugarcane juice
1 cup coconut milk
1 teaspoon finely ground star anise

Scoop the flesh out of the passion fruit and place it in a mixing bowl.

Add the condensed milk, sugarcane juice, coconut milk, and 1 cup of crushed ice and combine in a cocktail shaker. Pour into glasses and serve immediately, sprinkled with star anise.

Cucumber Pineapple Cooler

This smooth drink is like nectar poured into glasses, with the tropical flavors of coconut and pineapple lending their sweetness to refreshing cucumber. The spicy undertones of ginger add a seductive aroma to this drink.

MAKES 4 TO 6 CUPS
3 cups cucumber, coarsely chopped
2 stalks celery, coarsely chopped, plus more for garnish
3 cups fresh pineapple juice
1 tablespoon fresh ginger juice

Place the cucumber, celery, pineapple juice, and ginger juice in a blender or a food processor and blend until smooth.

Garnish with the celery stalks and serve chilled over ice.

Ginger Elderflower Lassi

A creative variation of the classic Indian smoothie, which is the cooling drink of the summer. The elderflower syrup adds tangy-sweet floral notes of flavor alongside the smoky taste and aroma of roasted cumin.

MAKES 4 CUPS
3 cups plain yogurt
1 tablespoon elderflower syrup
One 1-inch fresh ginger, peeled and sliced
½ teaspoon cumin seeds, roasted and ground
Pinch of salt
Pinch of sugar
1 teaspoon black pepper, coarsely ground

Place yogurt, elderflower syrup, ginger, cumin seeds, salt, and sugar in a blender with 1 cup of ice and ½ cup of water and blend until smooth.

Serve in a glass, sprinkled with black pepper.

Dried Fruit Milkshake with Cardamom Scent

This drink is a wonderful welcome to guests for any occasions. I sometimes prefer to serve it warm for gatherings in winter as it makes for a nutritious and comforting beverage on a cold dreary day.

MAKES 4 TO 6 CUPS
3 cups whole milk
10 dried dates, pitted, preferably Medjool
4 dried figs
⅓ cup golden raisins
6 to 8 dried prunes
1 tablespoon honey, or to taste
1 teaspoon cardamom powder
2 tablespoons almonds, thinly sliced

Combine the milk, dates, figs, raisins, prunes, honey, and cardamom in a blender and blend until smooth.

Garnish with almonds and serve.

Hibiscus and Vanilla Iced Tea

This is my version of the classic Jamaican hibiscus iced tea, which is traditionally made with fresh hibiscus flowers. But you can also make this drink with dried flowers of the same robust color and flavors. The hibiscus gives the tea a beautiful pinkish-red hue and herbal fragrance, which is infused with the enticing flavors of vanilla. This recipe is perfect for hot summer days.

MAKES 4 TO 6 CUPS
1 vanilla pod
½ cup sugar, or to taste
⅓ cup dried hibiscus flowers
One 1-inch fresh ginger, peeled and crushed
2 lemons, cut into wedges

Slice open the vanilla pod and scrape out the insides with the back of a knife.

Place 1 cup of water in a small saucepan and add the vanilla seeds, empty pod, sugar, hibiscus, and ginger. Heat gently over low heat, stirring until the sugar is dissolved. Remove from the heat, cover, and let rest for at least 30 minutes to blend all the flavors.

Strain, then stir in the lemon wedges and let cool.

Add chilled water to the mixture, pour over ice, and serve.

Lavender and Cucumber Crush

The floral aroma of purple lavender soothes, refreshes, and brings memories of fragrant fields in the summer. Sometimes I like to add a scoop of lemon sorbet to this drink. You can strain out the lavender or leave it in for great presentation.

MAKES 4 TO 6 CUPS
Rind from 2 lemons
1 tablespoon fresh ginger juice
10 lavender flower heads
4 cardamom pods, lightly crushed
1 cup sugar
1 cucumber, cut into ⅓-inch roundels

Place the lemon rind, ginger juice, lavender, cardamom, sugar, and 1½ cups of hot water in a medium pot. Bring it to a boil on high heat. Reduce the heat to low, cover, and cook for 2 to 3 minutes. Remove from the heat and let it stand for 30 to 40 minutes at room temperature.

Refrigerate and cool the syrup. Mix with water or seltzer and serve over ice, garnished with the cucumber.

Strawberry Tea Smoothie

This drink is inspired by the green tea–flavored frozen yogurt blended with the goodness of berries. If mangoes are in season, add the pulp of one mango to create another dimension of flavor.

MAKES 4 CUPS
4 green tea bags, or any other herbal tea
2 cups plain yogurt
2 cups strawberries, hulled and coarsely chopped, plus more for garnish
2 tablespoons honey

Combine 1 cup of water with the green tea and bring it to a boil. Reduce the heat and simmer for 1 more minute and remove from the heat to cool.

Strain and refrigerate until chilled.

Transfer the yogurt, strawberries, honey, and tea to a blender and process until smooth.

Cover and chill in a refrigerator.

Serve garnished with a strawberry.

Rambutan, Mulberry, and Rose Water

Drinks offer a great degree of versatility without too much effort. You can use whichever fruits and vegetables are in season and combine them to make interesting blends. Similar to lychees, rambutan has a characteristic tropical sweet-subtle flavor. Be sure not to add too much rose water, or else it will overpower the taste of the fruits.

SERVES 4
2 to 3 pounds rambutan, peeled and pitted
Few drops rose water
½ cup mulberries
1 lemon, cut into wedges

Put the rambutan through a juice extractor. Stir in the rose water. Pour into a glass half filled with ice, add chilled water, and serve immediately, garnished with mulberries and lemon wedges.

Winter Cardamom Mocha

This drink combines my two favorite flavors, coffee and chocolate. Cardamom is yet another essential ingredient that creates a surprising and memorable accent in this drink. I prefer using dark, intense, good-quality bittersweet chocolate.

MAKES 4 CUPS

4 tablespoons sugar, or to taste
¼ cup unsweetened cocoa powder
2 cups whole milk
1 teaspoon cardamom seeds, finely ground
4 ounces bittersweet chocolate, finely grated
1 cup brewed coffee

Combine 1 cup of water, sugar, cocoa powder, milk, cardamom, 3 ounces of chocolate, and coffee and bring to a boil on medium high heat. Reduce the heat to low, stirring continuously. Simmer for 2 to 3 minutes, until all the flavors are well combined.

Serve hot, sprinkled with the reserved grated chocolate.

Pomegranate Honey Tofu Smoothie

Along with the tart flavors of pomegranate juice, silken tofu is added to this recipe to make a thick and smooth drink packed with proteins and antioxidants. I prefer using soft rather than firm tofu to achieve the right consistency for this drink.

SERVES 4
3 cups pomegranate juice
1 cup soft tofu
2 tablespoons honey, plus more to taste
1 cup plain yogurt
One 1-inch fresh ginger, peeled and finely chopped
½ cup fresh pomegranate seeds

Combine the pomegranate juice, tofu, honey, yogurt, and ginger in a blender or food processor. Purée until smooth.

Refrigerate until chilled and serve garnished with fresh pomegranate seeds.

ACKNOWLEDGMENTS

"I dream my painting and I paint my dream" was the belief of Vincent van Gogh. Similarly I dreamt of doing a great vegetarian cookbook for years and wanted to create it just like a painting. It was like "I dream of a cookbook and I cook like a dream." But the true reflection of the book was in the title of the Indian edition, *Hymns from the Soil*. A chef's tribute to the most essential element of life—soil.

I first want to thank all my gurus at home, who were all vegetarians and taught me the true power of food. The best part of my childhood was shelling peas, learning how to chop onions without crying, waiting every day to see a new blossom of vegetable or a sprout grow in my garden, and of course climbing the mango trees in summer. It was all about learning how to love to eat bitter gourds and of course enjoying the legacy of India's vegetarian cuisine. India is an ocean of vegetarian cuisine, and the varieties and traditions to cook them are almost infinite. I thank so many home cooks who have inspired me to cook vegetables in the most interesting ways.

When I used to work as a teenager at my Lawrence Gardens, I used to clean the kitchen and prepare all the vegetables myself for the next day. Sometimes I would be very late and see my Biji sitting in the verandah, waiting for me to finish; sometimes she would be dozing off or sometimes she would be chanting her mantra with a rosary in her hand. It somehow kept me safe.

While I was writing this book, we worked hours with the team of Chef Michael Swamy who photographed every dish, creating immortal frames of taste. You guys are brilliant. Ganesh Shedge, I feel so proud of your talents and may you grow forever and shine. Special thanks to Nokia for introducing me to the Lumia 1020 for capturing the images in this book.

Chef Varun Inamdar and Hanif Sheikh; the aromas of your cooking crossed every border as we were testing the recipes. Mugdha Savkar for helping me at every step of creating the recipes. Jyoti Mehrotra from Bloomsbury for being with me for every detail of the book. You are truly a dream editor-friend for every author. My special thanks to Poonam Kaul, Kavneet Sahni from Culinary Communications, Karan Sandhu, Gaurav Bajaj, and Armaan Dhir for all your support. My sincere thanks to Chef Arti Thapa and Chef Navdeep Sharma for inspiring me to create this book.

While we were designing this book at Kam Studio with Kamlesh Hiranandani and Maninder Singh and team for hours and hours, Suresh Gopal ji sat outside silently, almost in a meditative mode. His being there was an assurance for me that this book would be safe and one day become yours.

Everything in life is a thread and culture is created with the continuation of this thread of traditions. As I grow older, I feel the reflection of this culture in my nieces, Ojasvi and Saumya, and I feel the strength of the bond that culture creates. I feel proud to be a part of this continuation through the Mothers—Meri Ma and Dharti Ma…my Mother and Mother Earth and I bow to both of you since you both represent Hymns from the Soil for me.

(Gonkhang) Chapel
of protective deities

GLOSSARY

Asafoetida Hing

Avocado Makkhan Phal

Basil Seeds Tukmaria

Bay Leaf Tej Patta

Black Cardamom Badi Elaichi

Black Cumin Seeds Shahi Jeera

Black Mustard Seeds Rai

Black Pepper Kali Mirch

Black Salt Kala Namak

Butter Makkhan

Carom Seeds Ajwain

Cayenne Chili Lal Mirch

Chickpeas Channa

Chili Powder Lal Mirch Powder

Cinnamon Dal Chini

Clarified Butter Ghee

Cloves Laung

Coconut Nariyal ka Choora/Boora

Coconut Dry Sukha Nariyal

Coriander Powder Dhania Powder

Coriander Seeds Sabut Dhania

Cumin Seeds Jeera

Curry Leaves Kari Patta

Dry Fenugreek Leaves Kasoori Methi

Dry Ginger Saunth

Dry Mango Powder Amchur

Dry Pomegranate Seeds Anardana

Fennel Seeds Saunf

Fenugreek Methi

Fenugreek Seeds Methi Dana

Fresh Coriander Hara Dhaniya

Fresh Ginger Adrak

Garlic Lasan

Green Cardamom Hari or Choti Elaichi

Green Chili Hari Mirch

Holy Basil Tulsi

Jaggery Gur

Kokum Bhirnda

Lentils Daal

Lime Nimboo

Lotus Root Nadru

Mace Javitri

Milk Doodh

Mint Pudina

Mustard Seeds Sarson

Nutmeg Jaiphal

Onion Payaz

Onion Seeds Kalonji

Peanuts Moongphalli

Poppy Seeds Khus Khus

Raisins Kish Mish

Red Chili Lal Mirch

Saffron Kesar

Sesame Seeds Til

Spinach Palak

Star Anise Chakriphool

Stoneflower Patthar Phool

Tamarind Imli

Turmeric Haldi

Vetiver Kewra

Vinegar Sirka

Water Pani

Yogurt Dahi

INDEX

IT TAKES A MILLION HANDS TO FEED A CHILD...

From the strong hand that ploughs to the precise hands that sow
From the loving hand that waters and waits for the sprout to grow
From the nimble hand that cleans to the rough hands that grinds
From the experienced hand that packs to the vendor's hand that binds
From the sturdy hand that kneads to the practiced hand that rolls
From the careful hand that begins to cook and nurtures our souls
And finally to that loving wrinkled hand which gently breaks away
A little piece of bread and blows cold air to make it cool every day
And begins to tell the folklore of imaginary sparrows that flew afar
To the immortal heroes, angels, and fairies that live on a distant star
The mythical men who attained magical strength when they ate
She ran after the little princess everywhere, still holding the plate
Then a little mind that travels a distant journey and suddenly stops
And a little morsel is eaten, completing the journey of divine crops
Even God's mothers also had to run after them for this sacred chase
A new Sun brings a new cycle of love, full of gratitude and grace
It takes a million hands to feed a child...

Vikas Khanna